I0559805

LEADERSHIP REBORN
STUDY GUIDE

8 Ways Faith Transforms Your Everyday Leadership

LARRY ELY AND DANIEL ELY

LEADERSHIP
BOOKS

Copyright ©2025 by Larry Ely and Daniel Ely.
Leadership Reborn Study Guide: 8 Ways Faith Transforms Your Everyday Leadership.
Published by Leadership Books, Inc. Las Vegas, NV – New York, NY
LeadershipBooks.com

ISBN 9781965401309 (Paperback)

Category: Christian Living, Spiritual Growth, Leadership

All Rights Reserved. No part of this publication may be reproduced, distributed, or transmitted in any form or by any means, including photocopying, recording, or other electronic or mechanical methods without the prior written permission of the publisher, except in the case of brief quotations embodied in critical reviews and certain other noncommercial uses permitted by copyright law.

Leadership Books, Inc. is committed to publishing works of quality and integrity. In that spirit, we are proud to offer this book to our readers; however, the story, the experiences, and the words are the authors alone. The conversations in the book all come from the author's recollections, not word-for-word transcripts. All of the events are true to the best of the author's memory. The author, in no way, represents any company, corporation, or brand mentioned herein. The views expressed are solely those of the author.

Scripture quotations marked, (NLT) are taken from the *Holy Bible*, New Living Translation, copyright ©1996, 2004, 2015 by Tyndale House Foundation. Used by permission of Tyndale House Publishers, Carol Stream, Illinois 60188. All rights reserved.

Scripture quotations marked, (NIV) are taken from the Holy Bible, New International Version®, NIV®. Copyright © 1973, 1978, 1984, 2011 by Biblica, Inc.™ Used by permission of Zondervan. All rights reserved worldwide. www.zondervan.com The "NIV" and "New International Version" are trademarks registered in the United States Patent and Trademark Office by Biblica, Inc.™

CONTENTS

INTRO

Leading others is challenging, making it hard to figure out the best way to lead and to do it well. With all the busyness and stress that comes with leadership, it can be difficult to keep our faith central. Can you relate to the following struggles that leaders face?

In today's culture, everyday leaders face challenging times:

- **Church leaders** struggle to lead their ministries and teams well at a time when the needs of the community are very high, and people are hurting.
- **Business leaders** struggle to manage profit, people, and principles in a success-driven culture.
- **Educators** struggle to lead their schools and students well with limited funding and high expectations.
- **Parents** wrestle with how to lead their kids and families well in a biblically hostile world.
- **Coaches** and players find it difficult to lead their teams well when the pressure to win is high and individual player success threatens to pull the team apart.
- **Students** struggle to lead their peers well when popularity, social media, and the stress of life rub against their faith.

All of these struggles make it hard for the everyday leader to navigate how to integrate their faith into their leadership.

As authors, we have been church leaders, business leaders, educators, parents, coaches, and students, and we know how challenging it is to lead well. Leading well is hard work with many obstacles, but it is possible to lead with faith and to overcome these challenges. We empathize with those of you on the front lines of leadership and in the leadership trenches trying to keep Christ at the center of your lives.

Would you like to become an even better leader and improve your leadership, enhance your effectiveness, and increase your impact with a faith-centered approach? We hope you do because this course is full of practical principles on leading well that relate to your leadership within your company, team, church, school, or family. Investing in your own leadership development is a great decision with huge benefits for you and the people around you. So, let's jump right in!

STUDY GUIDE OVERVIEW

PURPOSE: This study guide is designed to be used alongside the *Leadership Reborn* video course. As you watch each video session, follow along in the study guide, take notes, highlight important ideas, go deeper into the topic, and answer the application questions.

THE FLOW OF EACH MAIN SESSION
(Most sessions follow this format)

1. **THE STORY:** This sets up the theme and topic.

2. **THE MAIN IDEAS:** These are the 5 major points from the video.

3. **THE WORD:** This is the featured Bible text for the topic.

4. **THE POINT:** This is the main focus of the section.

5. **THE CHANGE:** This is how faith changes your leadership.

6. **THE SPOTLIGHT:** This is a highlight of leadership in action.

7. **THE APPLICATION:** This is where you put it all into practice.

SESSION 1
LEADERSHIP BASICS

KEY QUESTION: Why Faith-Based Leadership?

STORY: The Solar System
- Leadership is like a solar system. Often, there is a central idea or principle that all the other aspects of leadership orbit around.
- Having the right center of our leadership makes all the difference.
- When the Son is at the center of our leadership, everything changes.

WHY DO WE NEED FAITH-BASED LEADERSHIP?
- There is a BIG difference between having faith as one of many principles that guide our leadership and having faith at the center of our leadership infusing all aspects of how we lead.

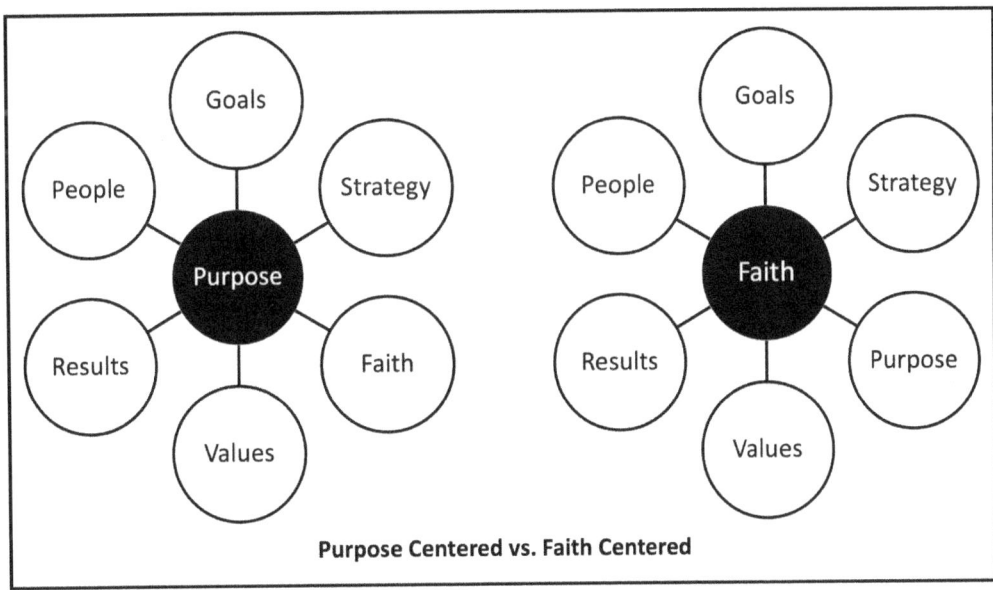

Purpose Centered vs. Faith Centered

Purpose Centered Model
- In this model, your faith may assist you, but it is not the driving force, and it does not inform the other areas of your leadership. This model works to varying degrees, but there is a better approach.

Faith Centered Model

- A faith-centered approach has more power, acceleration, and torque for the long haul. We can often accomplish more with God's strength fueling us, His principles guiding us, and His Spirit empowering us than we can on our own.

The Struggle of Many Models

1. Many models put other things at the center of their leadership.
2. Most traditional leadership models don't address the problem of human nature.
3. Many traditional models can be difficult to sustain.

LEADERSHIP REBORN: Faith changes our leadership by providing…

- A divine <u>motivation</u> and <u>purpose</u>
- A *reprioritizing* of <u>values</u>
- A *reforming* of effective <u>strategies</u>
- A *releasing* of <u>power</u>
- A *renewed* sense of <u>perspective</u>
- A *redefined* view of <u>success</u>
- A *redistribution* of <u>credit</u>

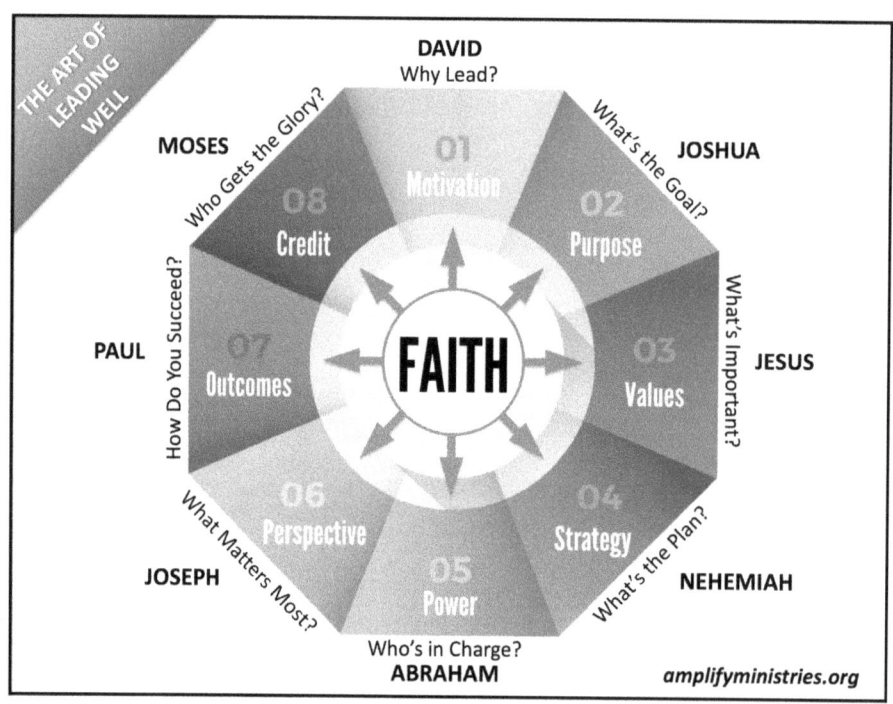

WHAT IS FAITH-BASED LEADERSHIP?

- Faith-based leadership is a personal leadership model, but it can also be a company or team model.
- Faith-based leadership is a biblical approach that begins with making God the leader of your life.
- Faith in God doesn't solve every leadership problem, but it makes a strong foundation on which to build better leadership.

A WHOLE PERSON APPROACH TO LEADERSHIP

- Leading well requires a whole person approach to leadership that involves all four aspects of a person: heart, mind, body, and soul.

HEART: The Character of a Leader

The character of a leader is who you are on the inside.

- Are you a moral and ethical person?
- Do you live and lead with integrity?
- Do you have a good heart and pure motives?
- Are you a good role model for others?

MIND: The Thinking of a Leader

The thinking of a leader is about your mindset, thoughts, and perspective.

- Do you give careful thought and attention to your leadership?
- Are you intentional, purposeful, and strategic in your planning?
- Do you consider the consequences, pros/cons, costs, and benefits?
- Do you seek the wisdom of others to guide your thinking and choices?

BODY: The Actions of a Leader

- The actions of a leader are how we actually lead and what we actually do.
- Do you lead by example?
- Do you consistently take action, accomplish tasks, and get involved?
- Do you inspire, motivate, cast vision, and communicate well?
- Do you set goals for your team and help them succeed?

SOUL: The Faith of a Leader

The faith of a leader is the spiritual aspect of a person that fuels and guides the heart, mind, and body.

- Is faith central to how you lead?
- Do you rely on God for strength, wisdom, and guidance?
- Do you invest in your own spiritual growth?
- Do you care about the spiritual health and well-being of the people you lead?

How They Work Together

- All four aspects are essential and work together in synchrony. Each one is affected by the others and creates harmony or discord depending on how we cultivate them.

THE APPLICATION: PUTTING IT INTO PRACTICE

- Reflect, discuss, and apply the following questions as they relate to your leadership within your company, team, church, school, or family.

1. What are some of your current official and unofficial leadership roles?

_____

_____

2. How would you rate or describe your current leadership in regard to your: heart (character), mind (thinking), body (actions), and soul (faith)?

Heart: _____

Mind: _____

Body: _____

Soul: _____

3. What role does faith play in your current style of leadership?

_____

_____

4. Have you ever experienced good leadership? What made it good?

_____

_____

5. Have you ever experienced bad leadership? What made it bad?

_____

_____

6. What are some of your strengths and weaknesses as a leader?

_____

_____

7. Who would benefit if you became an even better leader than you already are?

_____

_____

8. What would it take for you to embrace faith as the central element of your leadership?

_____

_____

KEY QUESTION: Why Lead?
FEATURED LEADER: David

THE STORY: Vince Lombardi

- Coach Vince Lombardi is considered one of the greatest motivators in football. He knew the key to motivating his team was to win their hearts.

- What motivates you to lead?

- Motivations for leading vary widely, but they usually follow our passions.

- Leading well begins with the right motivations and having the right heart.

OVERVIEW

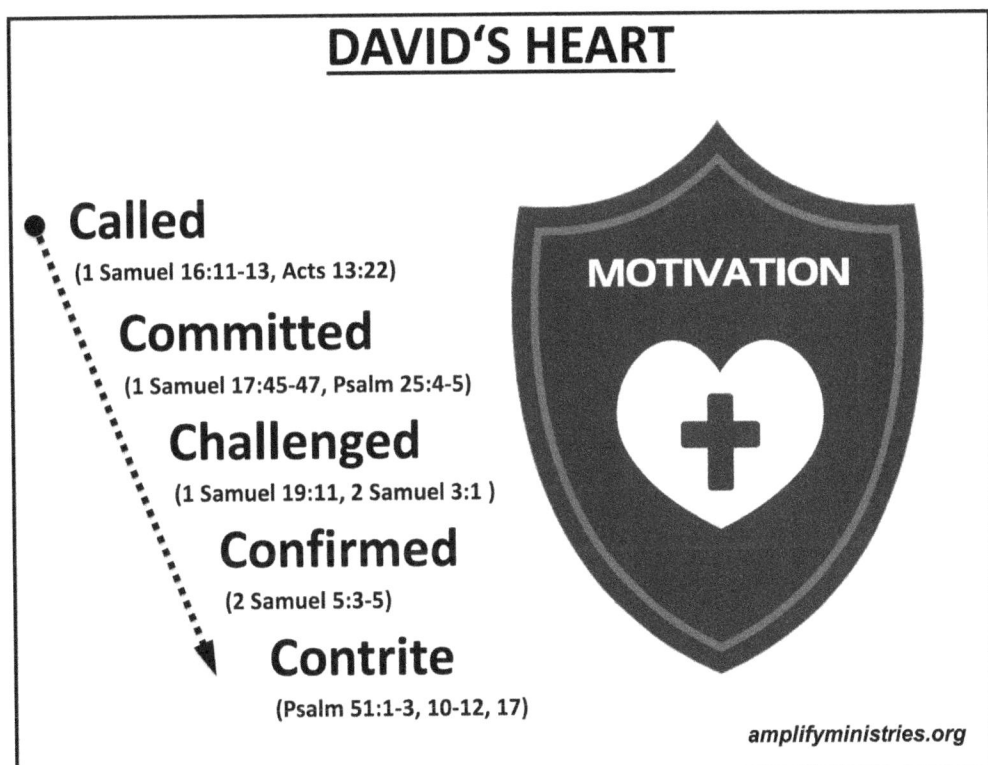

DAVID'S HEART

Called
(1 Samuel 16:11-13, Acts 13:22)

Committed
(1 Samuel 17:45-47, Psalm 25:4-5)

Challenged
(1 Samuel 19:11, 2 Samuel 3:1)

Confirmed
(2 Samuel 5:3-5)

Contrite
(Psalm 51:1-3, 10-12, 17)

MOTIVATION

amplifyministries.org

1. CALLED TO LEAD

- If a friend or someone important asked you to take a leadership role, would you do it? What if God was the one inviting you to lead?

- David was called to lead at a young age, most likely as a teenager. God saw potential in him and knew he had the right heart to eventually lead His people.

THE WORD

- *"After removing Saul, he made David their king. God testified concerning him: 'I have found David son of Jesse, a man after my own heart; he will do everything I want him to do.'"* (Acts 13:22, NIV)

- **Go Deeper:** 1 Samuel 16:11-13

THE POINT

- David feared and followed the Lord, and his heart was in the right place.

- Faith-based leadership begins with an open heart toward God and a willingness to follow His leading in our lives.

- How will you respond or have you responded to God when prompted to lead or take a leadership role?

NOTES

LEADERSHIP REBORN

2. COMMITTED TO GOD

- One of the best things about David was his commitment to God.

- David heard the giant, Goliath, taunting and insulting the Israelite forces, and he was bothered that no one went out to silence the enemy's threats against God's people.

- David stepped up to the challenge when no one else did, and he trusted God to give him victory in battle when all the odds were stacked against him.

THE WORD

- *"David replied to the Philistine, "You come to me with sword, spear, and javelin, but I come to you in the name of the LORD of Heaven's Armies—the God of the armies of Israel, whom you have defied."* (1 Samuel 17:45, NLT)

- **Go Deeper:** 1 Samuel 17:45-47, 2 Samuel 6:12b, 6:15, Psalm 25:4-5

THE POINT

- As king, David showed his commitment to the Lord by bringing back the Ark of the Covenant to Jerusalem and demonstrated to the people that worship was central.

- David's commitment to follow God for the long haul set him apart as a strong leader.

- We can't lead well if our hearts are in the wrong place.

- We must push aside our selfish desires, resist the things that distract our hearts, and be steadfast in our commitment to God above all else.

NOTES

LEADERSHIP REBORN

3. CHALLENGED TO GIVE UP

- God promised David he would become king of Israel, but God's timing remained a mystery.
- David's road to becoming king was filled with many roadblocks and significant obstacles that blocked his path.
- Enemies, division, assassination attempts, and war, all threatened to undermine David and end his life or cause him to give up.
- The roadblocks in David's life continually challenged him to give up and abandon his leadership journey and God's calling on his life.

THE WORD

- *"The war between the house of Saul and the house of David lasted a long time. David grew stronger and stronger, while the house of Saul grew weaker and weaker." (2 Samuel 3:1, NIV)*
- **Go Deeper:** 1 Samuel 19:11a, 23:14-15, 2 Samuel 2:10

THE POINT

- The temptations to quit, to stop, to hide, to retreat, and to accept defeat were strong, yet David stood firm and resisted.
- Leading well requires a certain tenacity and grit in the face of opposition.
- It takes strong faith and bold determination to hold your ground, to plow ahead one difficult step at a time, and to take on the obstacles that block our path.
- Faith-based leadership clings to the promises of God in the face of adversity, holds fast to the calling God put in our hearts, locks arms with those around them, and trusts that if God has called us, then he will make a way.

NOTES

LEADERSHIP REBORN

4. CONFIRMED AS KING

- After overcoming many obstacles in his path, David became king of Judah at the age of thirty.
- He reigned over this smaller region for seven years, before he finally became king of all Israel and reigned for thirty-three years.

THE WORD

- *"David was thirty years old when he began to reign, and he reigned forty years in all." (2 Samuel 5:4, NLT)*
- **Go Deeper:** 2 Samuel 5:3-5

THE POINT

- David's confirmation as king of Judah and Israel points to God's faithfulness over time.
- David's heart for God opened the door for God to use him in some amazing ways, and the nation of Israel prospered under his rule.
- Leading well starts with having a heart for God and then embracing the leadership opportunities that God brings along.

NOTES

LEADERSHIP REBORN

5. CONTRITE AND OPEN-HEARTED

- Although David made many mistakes in his life and messed up publicly as a leader at times, he remained committed to his faith.

- He continued to be open-hearted toward God, and contrite about his sins.

- Clearly, his heart went astray for a time.

- When confronted with his shortcomings, David confessed, repented, and kept a soft heart toward God.

THE WORD

- *"Create in me a pure heart, O God, and renew a steadfast spirit within me." (Psalm 51:10, NIV)*
- **Go Deeper:** Psalm 51:1-3, 51:10-12, 51:17, Proverbs

THE POINT

- What made David a great leader was his heart for God, his faithful devotion to the Lord, and his willingness to continually come back to God when he made mistakes.

- Faith-based leadership involves surrendering your heart to God and then protecting your heart from going astray.

- Leading well over the course of time requires a diligent guarding of our hearts that involves repeatedly focusing and refocusing on the Lord.

NOTES

LEADERSHIP REBORN

THE CHANGE

- How does infusing faith into our leadership affect our motivation?
- Faith reframes our motivation, why we lead, and how we motivate others in three key ways.

1. Leading well starts with the leader's heart.
2. Our faith adds a spiritual aspect to why we lead.
3. Faith changes how we motivate others.

THE SPOTLIGHT: JOHN F. KENNEDY AND PT-109

- During WWII, John F. Kennedy was a Lieutenant in the Navy. While on patrol, his boat was rammed and destroyed by an enemy ship.
- Crisis tests our leadership and the struggle to survive pushes us to our limits.
- Kennedy's actions resemble David's leadership in regard to his heart and commitment to his men, motivating his crew under adverse conditions, being challenged to give up, and overcoming obstacles.
- Leading well incorporates all these things and often asks more of ourselves than we ever thought possible.

THE APPLICATION: PUTTING IT INTO PRACTICE

- Reflect, discuss, and apply the following questions as they relate to your leadership within your company, team, church, school, or family.

1. How's your heart? Is it open to God and His leading in your life? Explain.

_____

_____

2. What motivates you to lead, and in what areas do you feel called to leadership?

_____

_____

3. What are some positive ways that you can motivate and inspire the people you lead?

_____

_____

4. How does infusing faith into your leadership affect your motivation to lead?

_____

_____

5. What are some of the challenging obstacles that you have faced in your leadership and how did you navigate them?

_____

_____

MY BIG TAKEAWAYS

1. _____

2. _____

3. _____

LEADERSHIP REBORN

SESSION 3
CHANGE IN PURPOSE

KEY QUESTION: What's the Goal?

FEATURED LEADER: Joshua

THE STORY: Apollo 13

- The Apollo 13 space mission to the moon didn't go as planned. It had a drastic change in purpose.
- The Apollo 13 mission shifted their goals from moon exploration to rescuing the crew.
- Life has a way of shifting our goals suddenly and forcing us to adapt to new situations.
- Faith changes our leadership goals and allows God to use our leadership for a bigger purpose.

OVERVIEW

JOSHUA'S GOAL

Cause (Joshua 1:1-5)

Courage (Joshua 1:6-9)

Character (Joshua 4:19-24)

Conviction (Joshua 6:1-7, 20)

Covenant (Joshua 8:30-32, 34-35)

PURPOSE

amplifyministries.org

1. CAUSE TO BELIEVE IN

- There is something powerful about a compelling cause.
- God calls Joshua to a leadership role and gives him the compelling cause of establishing a new homeland for the people of Israel.
- Joshua inspires his people and his army to action.

THE WORD

- *"Moses my servant is dead. Therefore, the time has come for you to lead these people, the Israelites, across the Jordan River into the land I am giving them."* *(Joshua 1:2, NLT)*
- **Go Deeper:** Joshua 1:1-5, Genesis 15:18-21

THE POINT

- Following in Moses' footsteps must have been intimidating and challenging.
- Joshua is tasked with conquering the Promised Land.
- He rises to the challenge, takes up the cause, and accepts the new position.

NOTES

_____

_____

_____

_____

_____

LEADERSHIP REBORN

2. COURAGE TO LEAD

- As the torch of leadership passed from Moses to Joshua, fear began to rise within Joshua.

- The pressure and weight of having to lead and be responsible for all of the Israelite people must have been heavy.

- Joshua needed the Lord's encouragement to be strong and courageous.

THE WORD

- *"This is my command—be strong and courageous! Do not be afraid or discouraged. For the LORD your God is with you wherever you go." (Joshua 1:9, NLT)*

- **Go Deeper:** Joshua 1:6-9

THE POINT

- It takes courage to lead well. Leadership can be scary, and fear can be paralyzing.

- God calls Joshua out of his fear and challenges him to be courageous.

- Often, good leaders have to swallow hard and face their own internal fears, summon their bravery, and take a leap of faith.

- Joshua courageously embraced his new role and overcame his fear and discouragement.

NOTES

LEADERSHIP REBORN

3. CHARACTER TO HONOR GOD

- Without strength of character, our leadership is open to corruption.

- Pride, ego, greed, and power can quickly sabotage our leadership.

- It is amazing how a lack of character can destroy a leader's career and undermine his or her leadership effectiveness.

- Your character matters. It takes high morals and ethics to lead well.

THE WORD

- *"It was there at Gilgal that Joshua piled up the twelve stones taken from the Jordan River. Then Joshua said to the Israelites, "In the future your children will ask, 'What do these stones mean?' Then you can tell them, 'This is where the Israelites crossed the Jordan on dry ground.'"* (Joshua 4:20-22, NLT)

- **Go Deeper:** Joshua 4:19-24

THE POINT

- Joshua had strong character that was rooted in a deep desire to honor God.

- Joshua used these twelve stones from the river to set up a memorial to the Lord. In doing so, Joshua pointed the people toward God and not his own ability.

- In the days ahead, when you doubt; when you forget; when you wonder, look at these rocks and remember what the Lord did.

NOTES

LEADERSHIP REBORN

4. CONVICTION TO FOLLOW THROUGH

- Sometimes God asks us to do strange things that we don't understand at the time.
- For Joshua and his army, the Battle of Jericho was one of those times.
- God asks them to march around the city walls of Jericho for seven days in full view of the enemy.

THE WORD

- *"On the seventh day you are to march around the town seven times, with the priests blowing the horns. When you hear the priests give one long blast on the rams' horns, have all the people shout as loud as they can. Then the walls of the town will collapse, and the people can charge straight into the town." (Joshua 6:4b-5, NLT)*
- **Go Deeper:** Joshua 6:1-7, 6:20

THE POINT

- Joshua obeyed the Lord's orders. It was an unconventional battle plan to say the least, but he didn't question his Commander and Chief.
- Joshua had the faith and conviction to follow through with what the Lord asked even when it didn't make sense to him. He trusted God, and God's battle plan.
- God showed up, and the walls of the city fell down. It was a miraculous victory.
- Leading well requires a deep conviction and trust in God.

NOTES

LEADERSHIP REBORN

5. COVENANT TO RENEW

- As Joshua switched gears from military commander to community leader, he built an altar on top of a mountain.

- He had the people of Israel participate in a type of covenant renewal ceremony with worship, teaching, and instruction.

- As the leader of God's special people, it was up to Joshua to help the Israelites fulfill the responsibilities and guidelines that God had given them.

THE WORD

- *"Joshua then read to them all the blessings and curses Moses had written in the Book of Instruction. Every word of every command that Moses had ever given was read to the entire assembly of Israel, including the women and children and the foreigners who lived among them."* (Joshua 8:34-35, NLT)
- **Go Deeper:** Joshua 8:30-32

THE POINT

- As leaders, getting everyone on the same page is a big deal, especially when leading a very large group of people.

- Having everyone participate in renewing their faith and accountability to God ensured there was no excuse for improper behavior or unclear expectations.

- Keeping God central in the hearts of the people was not easy, but it was an essential function of Joshua's leadership and ours.

NOTES

LEADERSHIP REBORN

THE CHANGE

- How does infusing faith into our leadership affect our purpose?

- Faith refocuses our purpose and the goal of our leadership in three ways by establishing a healthy spiritual life, private life, and community life.

1. Love God and honor him above all.
2. Strong inner character & integrity protect our effectiveness.
3. Leading well means caring for the hearts, souls, and lives of others.

THE SPOTLIGHT: THE EFFECTS OF COVID-19

- When COVID-19 hit in 2020, the world changed.
- Pharmaceutical companies ceased normal operations and began working on vaccines.

- COVID-19 caused people to re-evaluate their lives.

- Leading well requires that we re-evaluate our purpose from time to time and make sure that our leadership is in alignment with God's purposes.

THE APPLICATION: PUTTING IT INTO PRACTICE

- Reflect, discuss, and apply the following questions as they relate to your leadership within your company, team, church, school, or family.

1. Spiritual Life: How is your love for God reflected in your leadership?

_____

_____

2. Private Life: How would you describe your inner character, morals, and ethics?

_____

_____

3. Community Life: How do you show love to the people you lead and care for their hearts, souls, and lives?

_____

_____

4. How does infusing faith into your leadership affect your purpose?

_____

_____

5. How have you had to show courage in your leadership, and what might be a courageous next step to take?

_____

_____

MY BIG TAKEAWAYS

1. _____

2. _____

3. _____

LEADERSHIP REBORN

SESSION 4
CHANGE IN VALUES

KEY QUESTION: What's Important?
FEATURED LEADER: Jesus

THE STORY: Reality Television show "Undercover Boss"

- The CEO and owner of a company went "undercover" as a bottom-level employee at a restaurant. Another boss did the same thing at a zoo.

- The idea of the boss getting dirty and placing himself in the shoes of his employees in order to identify with them is an intriguing concept.

- There is an important leadership lesson that the TV show and the Bible both highlight and that is the VALUE of people.

OVERVIEW

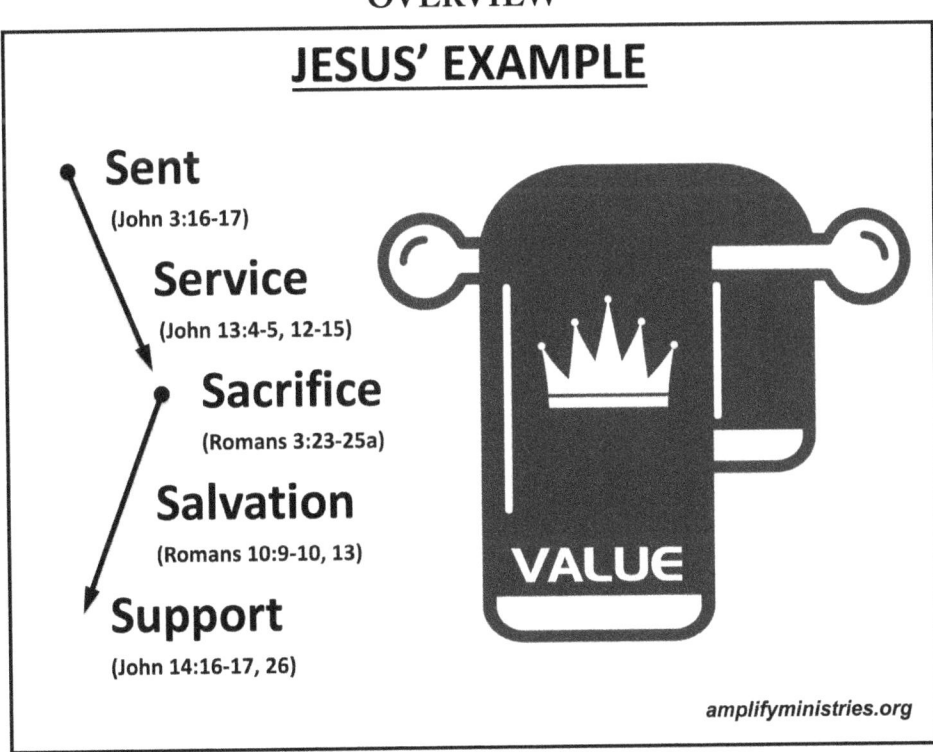

1. SENT BY GOD

- In many ways, Jesus was the original "Undercover Boss."
- Jesus came down from His throne in heaven to live among us as God's representative.
- Out of love for humanity, God sent Jesus on a rescue mission to restore us back into a relationship with Himself.

THE WORD

- *"For God so loved the world that he gave his one and only Son, that whoever believes in him shall not perish but have eternal life." (John 3:16, NIV)*
- **Go Deeper:** John 1:14, 3:16-17

THE POINT

- You are loved by God. Jesus is proof of God's love for you.
- Every leader needs to know deep down that he or she is loved by God.
- Knowing and experiencing God's love frees us to lead and serve others.
- God sent Jesus. Now Jesus sends us.

NOTES

_____
_____
_____
_____
_____

LEADERSHIP REBORN

2. SERVICE TO OTHERS

- It is easy to be selfish. We are born that way. It is in our nature to be self-focused.
- Serving others is a learned behavior not an instinctual one, so it is important to have a good teacher.
- Jesus is the ultimate example of servant leadership.
- Jesus flipped the idea of top-down leadership over by setting aside his rightful throne and took on the nature of a servant.

THE WORD

- *"Don't be selfish; don't try to impress others. Be humble, thinking of others as better than yourselves. Don't look out only for your own interests, but take an interest in others, too." (Philippians 2:3–4, NLT)*
- **Go Deeper:** Philippians 2:3-8, John 13:4-5, 13:12-15

THE POINT

- Jesus is the Master teacher when it comes to putting other people's needs first.
- Jesus exchanged his crown for a towel as he washed the disciples' feet and taught them the value of serving and loving those around them.
- Jesus gives us a powerful example to follow, especially those in leadership.

BONUS: In my leadership context as a student pastor, I taught the following acronym to students to help them remember the value of serving others. Maybe, it will help you too.

S.E.R.V.E.

- **S** erve one another in love *(Galatians 5:3)*
- **E** verywhere you go *(Acts 1:8)*
- **R** ely on God's strength *(2 Corinthians 1:9, Psalm 46:1)*
- **V** alue others more than yourself *(Philippians 2:3)*
- **E** xpress God's love with your actions *(James 2:17, John 13:34)*

NOTES

LEADERSHIP REBORN

3. SACRIFICE FOR OTHERS

- Most people make small sacrifices all of the time.

- Leaders are no strangers to sacrifice: working late, taking the heat for the team, thankless effort, conflict resolution, and constant problem-solving.

- Many of us often sacrifice our time, money, energy, and sleep to get the job done. However, most leaders stop short of sacrificing their lives.

THE WORD

- *"He himself is the sacrifice that atones for our sins—and not only our sins but the sins of all the world." (1 John 2:2, NLT)*

- **Go Deeper:** John 17:19, Hebrews 9:28, Romans 3:23-25a

THE POINT

- For Jesus, the cost of leading was high. He made the ultimate sacrifice and gave His life for His followers, for you and me, and for the world.

- **Why did He do it?** He was the only one who could pay the price for our sins. He did it out of love.

- **What did He give up?** He gave up His status, throne, pride, dignity, and embraced humility. He gave up Himself in order to gain something greater.

- **Was it worth it?** Yes, through His sacrifice we are able to be forgiven and restored to God.

NOTES

LEADERSHIP REBORN

4. SALVATION FOR ALL

- Jesus was sent by God, served others, and sacrificed himself all for our salvation. His whole mission was designed to rescue us all.

- Most people don't believe they need saving. It is not easy to admit we need help; that we need someone to rescue us.

- If you really want to lead well, you have to deal with your shortcomings, confess your mistakes, and turn to God. Leading well requires faith.

- Salvation is available to anyone and everyone who puts their faith and trust in Jesus.

THE WORD

- *"If you confess with your mouth that Jesus is Lord and believe in your heart that God raised him from the dead, you will be saved." (Romans 10:9, NLT)*

- **Go Deeper:** Romans 10:9-10, 10:13, 1 Peter 3:18, 2 Timothy 3:15, Colossians 1:13-14

THE POINT

- Through Jesus' death and resurrection, He was able to provide forgiveness for all of our sins and restore us back to God.

- I ask you, leader to leader, have you put your faith in Jesus Christ? If so, that's awesome! If not, that's ok too, but I urge you to consider taking a step of faith.

- Respectfully, and if and when you are ready, here is a simplified way to begin your faith journey. It starts with these four words: love, rebellion, sacrifice, and faith.

LOVE   REBELLION   SACRIFICE   FAITH

- **God's LOVE:**
  He loves you *(John 3:16)*

- **Our REBELLION:**
  We all sin and make mistakes *(Romans 3:23)*

- **Jesus' SACRIFICE:**
  He died on the cross for your sins & rose again *(Romans 5:8)*

- **Our FAITH:**
  We believe and ask Him to forgive us *(1 John 1:9)*

amplifyministries.org

- **PRAYER OF FAITH**

  God, thank you for your love. Forgive me for my rebellion and sin. I accept Jesus' sacrifice on the cross as payment for my sins. I believe and put my faith in Jesus today. Amen.

- Putting our faith in Jesus is at the heart of faith-based leadership. It is not a requirement for leading, but our faith in Him makes our leadership better.

NOTES

LEADERSHIP REBORN

5. SUPPORT FOR HIS FOLLOWERS

- After He died on the cross, rose again, and returned to heaven, Jesus sent the Holy Spirit to guide us, to teach us, and to live within His followers.
- The Holy Spirit acts as a spiritual and moral conscience guiding us in how to live and act in order to please God and follow the Bible.

THE WORD

- *"But when the Father sends the Advocate as my representative—that is, the Holy Spirit—he will teach you everything and will remind you of everything I have told you." (John 14:26, NLT)*
- **Go Deeper:** John 14:16-17, Acts 1:8

THE POINT

- We are not alone, and we don't have to lead alone.
- God wants to help us lead as we rely on Him and the power of His Spirit to inform and guide our leadership decisions.
- Relying on God's strength and the guidance of the Holy Spirit is a daily choice that faith-based leaders must choose to follow or not.

NOTES

LEADERSHIP REBORN

THE CHANGE

- How does infusing faith into our leadership affect our values?
- Faith reprioritizes our values and what's important in three key ways.

1. Leading well requires biblical values at its core.
2. The value of people is paramount. Value people over profits, programs, and procedures.
3. Leadership at its base level is rooted in building healthy relationships.

THE SPOTLIGHT: CORE VALUES @ CHICK-FIL-A®

- People matter, and Chick-fil-A® knows it, believes it, and teaches it.
- For them, it wasn't just training, it was about doing business differently.
- Chick-fil-A® serves as a great example of a company that is driven by biblical values and is still wildly successful as a productive business.
- Chick-fil-A® shows us how a change in values can transform the way we lead.

THE APPLICATION: PUTTING IT INTO PRACTICE

- Reflect, discuss, and apply the following questions as they relate to your leadership within your company, team, church, school, or family.

1. How is Jesus' value system and leadership different from traditional models?

_____

_____

2. How can you build healthy relationships with the people and teams you lead and show them how valuable they are?

_____

_____

3. What does it look like to serve well and make sacrifices in your leadership context?

_____

_____

4. What biblical values are at the core of your leadership or need to be at the core?

_____

_____

5. If you have put your faith in Jesus, how has He changed your leadership? If you have not, what would it take for you to consider putting your faith in Jesus?

_____

_____

MY BIG TAKEAWAYS

1. _____

2. _____

3. _____

LEADERSHIP REBORN

SESSION 5
CHANGE IN STRATEGY

KEY QUESTION: What's the Plan?
FEATURED LEADER: Nehemiah

THE STORY: Women's Intramural Soccer Championship

- As the Taylor University Women's Intramural Soccer Championship kicked off, we realized our team was in trouble. We were outmatched.

- We needed a new strategy. We told our team to stop playing offense, and only play defense in the second half. We intentionally played for a shootout and won.

- Developing effective strategies is a core function of a leader, but not all strategies are worth implementing. Leaders must carefully weigh the pros and cons.

- Leading well requires that we allow our faith to guide the strategies that we choose and to pick honorable ones.

OVERVIEW

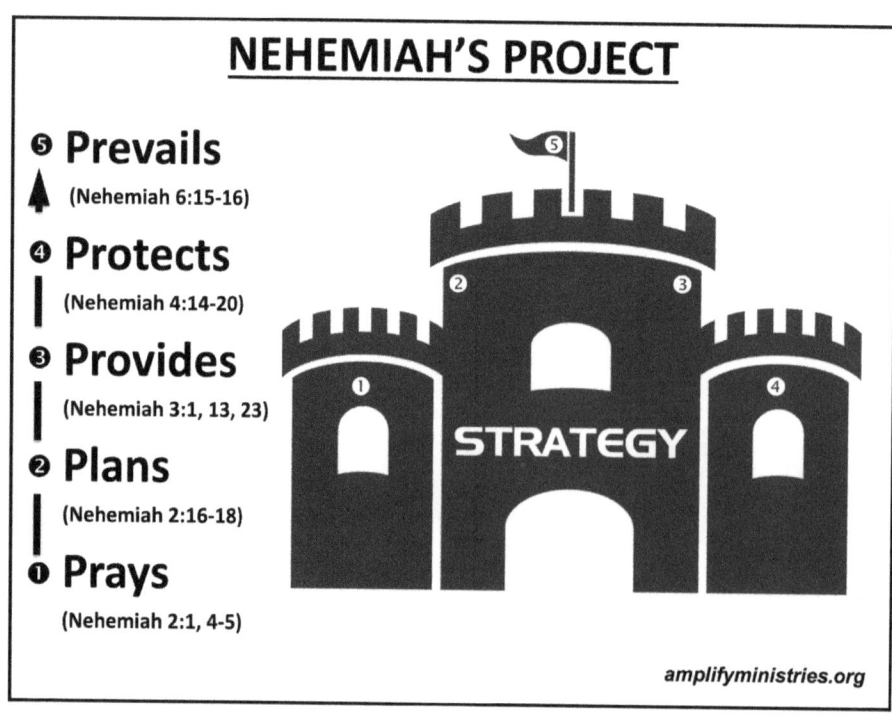

1. NEHEMIAH PRAYS

- When Nehemiah heard that the holy city of Jerusalem lay in ruins, he felt led by God to take on the massive project of rebuilding the city walls.
- Nehemiah began his project with prayer. He confessed the sins of his people and prayed for favor with the king.
- With the king's blessing, Nehemiah travels to Jerusalem to begin its restoration.

THE WORD

- *"The king asked, "Well, how can I help you?" With a prayer to the God of heaven, I replied, "If it please the king, and if you are pleased with me, your servant, send me to Judah to rebuild the city where my ancestors are buried." (Nehemiah 2:4-5, NLT)*

- **Go Deeper:** Nehemiah 2:1-5

THE POINT

- Prayer was an essential part of Nehemiah's leadership strategy as he continually relied on God and covered his project and his people in constant prayer.
- Nehemiah kept his focus by frequently asking God for help, provision, protection, and strength.
- Many leaders try to do things on their own strength, with their own drive, desires, and determination.
- Leading well starts with prayer and continues in prayer.

BONUS: PRAYERS OF NEHEMIAH

- **Prayer of Confession:** forgiveness and favor (1:4-11)
- **Prayer of Courage:** facing the king and requesting to leave (2:4)
- **Prayer of Punishment:** prays against his enemies (4:4-5)
- **Prayer of Protection:** protect our lives and the city (4:8-9)
- **Prayer of Blessing:** provide for me and bless me (5:19)
- **Prayer of Strength:** strengthen my hands to work (6:9)
- **Prayer of Justice:** remember my enemies and their actions (6:14)

NOTES

LEADERSHIP REBORN

2. NEHEMIAH PLANS

- Every good leader needs a plan. It is hard to be successful without one.

- Having a well-conceived plan was a big part of what made Nehemiah's strategy so effective.

- His plan began with: prayer, gaining the king's favor, gathering lumber and supplies, securing an armed escort, requesting traveling papers, and recon.

THE WORD

- *"But now I said to them, 'You know very well what trouble we are in. Jerusalem lies in ruins, and its gates have been destroyed by fire. Let us rebuild the wall of Jerusalem and end this disgrace!'"* (Nehemiah 2:17, NLT)

- **Go Deeper:** Nehemiah 2:11-18

THE POINT

- With his preparations complete, he then cast the vision to the Jewish leaders.

- Nehemiah's recruiting efforts were a success, and the leaders agreed to join him in the huge undertaking. Clearly the Lord's favor was upon Nehemiah.

- Nehemiah's careful planning paid off as more leaders, family groups, and tribesmen joined the project to rebuild the walls of the city.

NOTES

LEADERSHIP REBORN

3. NEHEMIAH PROVIDES

- Nehemiah's plan included providing three more vital aspects to the project. He provided delegation, communication, and ownership.

- **Delegation:** In order to complete the rebuilding quickly and efficiently he delegated the work to capable groups of people working together with a common goal.

- **Ownership:** He assigned people to rebuild sections of the wall behind and beside their own homes. In this way, Nehemiah gave the workers ownership and an incentive.

- **Communication:** Nehemiah's ability to communicate his plan clearly to the leaders and to the workers was one of the keys to the success of his project.

THE WORD

- *"The Valley Gate was repaired by the people from Zanoah, led by Hanun. They set up its doors and installed its bolts and bars. They also repaired the 1,500 feet of wall to the Dung Gate." (Nehemiah 3:13, NLT)*

- **Go Deeper:** Nehemiah 3:1, 3:23, 4:9-14, 5:6-7

THE POINT

- Great plans need great communication, ownership, and delegation.

- Poor communication has been the downfall of many organizations, teams, and families. A lack of ownership creates disinterest, and without delegation, the burden becomes too heavy to carry.

- Leading well means taking the time to communicate clearly, efficiently, and effectively with all the people that are involved.

NOTES

LEADERSHIP REBORN

4. NEHEMIAH PROTECTS

- As the rebuilding of the wall progressed, Nehemiah's opposition increased.
- It began with threats and distractions and culminated in surrounding regions preparing to attack them.
- He adapted his strategy and met the needs of his workers head-on.

THE WORD

- *"But from then on, only half my men worked while the other half stood guard with spears, shields, bows, and coats of mail. The leaders stationed themselves behind the people of Judah who were building the wall. The laborers carried on their work with one hand supporting their load and one hand holding a weapon." (Nehemiah 4:16-17, NLT)*
- **Go Deeper:** Nehemiah 4:14-20, 5:6-7, 5:9-12

THE POINT

- First, he dealt with the people's physical protection. He empowered them to keep working by posting guards and equipping the workers with weapons.
- A second enemy threatened the project from within, and Nehemiah had to pause to address infighting and injustice in his ranks.
- By addressing both the people's physical safety and economic concerns, Nehemiah was able to boost morale, gain respect, and build unity.
- Leading well means balancing the project goals and the people's needs.

NOTES

LEADERSHIP REBORN

---

5. NEHEMIAH PREVAILS

- In an amazing act of God and in record time, the walls and gates around the entire holy city were finished.

- With tremendous leadership, bravery, collaboration, perseverance, grit, and sheer hard work, the whole project was completed in less than two months.

THE WORD

- *"So the wall was completed on the twenty-fifth of Elul, in fifty-two days. When all our enemies heard about this, all the surrounding nations were afraid and lost their self-confidence, because they realized that this work had been done with the help of our God. (Nehemiah 6:15-16, NIV)*

- **Go Deeper:** Nehemiah 6:1-4, 7:1-3

THE POINT

- In the midst of adversity, Nehemiah's faith-based leadership shone brightly as the whole community prevailed, and the surrounding nations were filled with fear.

- Some leaders think that the end justifies the means, but that is not the case. Nehemiah prevailed, and his strategy honored God and the people.

- Leading well means choosing our strategies wisely because HOW we get there matters.

NOTES

LEADERSHIP REBORN

THE CHANGE

- How does infusing faith into our leadership affect how we develop strategies?

- Faith reforms our strategy and how we accomplish the plan in three key ways.

1. Our strategy must fit with the values and purposes of the Bible.
2. Invite God into the strategy development process.
3. Share the plan, delegate jobs, and release your team to do it.

THE SPOTLIGHT: VOLVO'S CHANGE IN STRATEGY

- Volvo's automobile assembly line struggled with production and morale.

- Volvo changed their strategy, and the assembly line was replaced with small groups of workers assembling the car in one area.

- Volvo's change in strategy is a great modern-day example of developing a plan to engage, equip, and empower its people.

THE APPLICATION: PUTTING IT INTO PRACTICE

- Reflect, discuss, and apply the following questions as they relate to your leadership within your company, team, church, school, or family.

1. Does your current leadership plan and strategy honor God and fit with the values and purposes of the Bible? Explain.

_____

_____

2. How can you better equip and empower people, delegate roles, and create ownership within your leadership context?

_____

_____

3. What are some ways that you can improve team communication, cooperation, and participation?

_____

_____

4. How does infusing faith into your leadership affect how you develop strategies?

_____

_____

5. Take a moment and invite God into the process. Pray over your strategies, plans, goals, co-workers, and teammates; ask God for His plan, provision, and protection.

_____

_____

MY BIG TAKEAWAYS

1. _____

2. _____

3. _____

LEADERSHIP REBORN

SESSION 6
CHANGE IN POWER

KEY QUESTION: Who's in Charge?

FEATURED LEADER: Abraham

THE STORY: Alexander the Great

- There is no room for power struggles or questioning authority on the battlefield.

- Alexander's soldiers followed his orders without question, even though it cost some of them their lives.

- Alexander the Great was in command and his soldiers and enemies knew it.

- Many of us struggle to trust God and surrender control of our lives to Him.

OVERVIEW

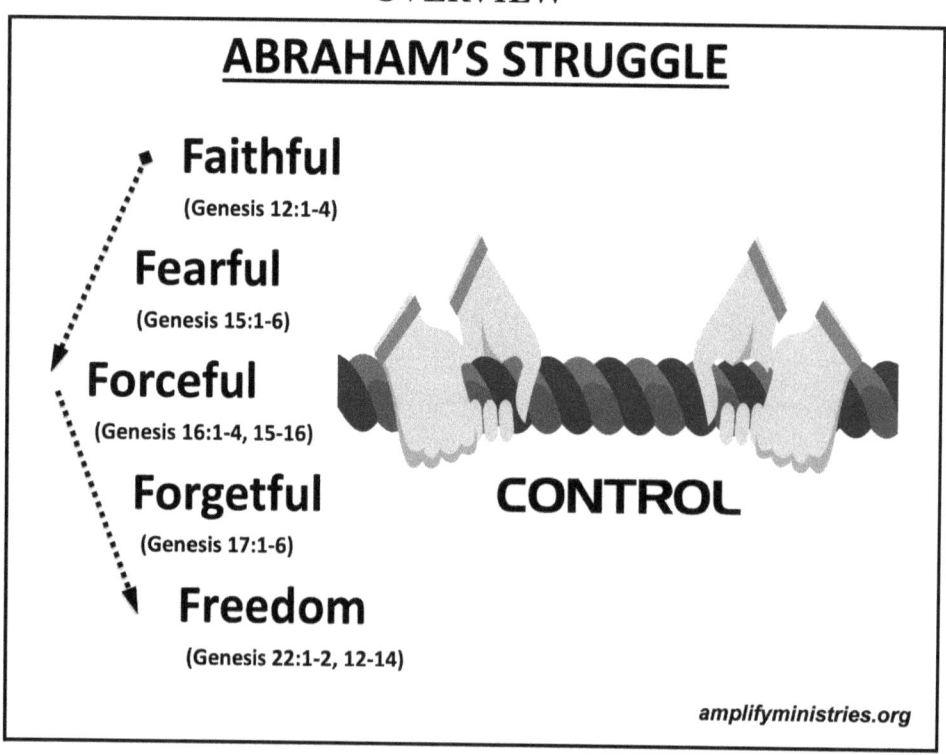

1. FAITHFUL TO FOLLOW

- There can be something exciting and exhilarating about exploring the unknown, but it can also be risky, dangerous, terrifying, and stressful.

- At the age of 75, Abram was called by God to pack up his stuff, take his family, leave his homeland, and travel to an unknown destination.

- Sometimes following God can be scary. Abram took a big leap of faith. He packed up his belongings, gathered his family, and went.

THE WORD

- *"The LORD had said to Abram, 'Leave your native country, your relatives, and your father's family, and go to the land that I will show you. I will make you into a great nation. I will bless you and make you famous, and you will be a blessing to others.'" (Genesis 12:1-2, NLT)*

- **Go Deeper:** Genesis 12:1-4

THE POINT

- Abram trusted God and was faithful to follow Him.

- It is hard to give up control. For most of us, it can be very unsettling. However, sometimes God asks us to do things that actually require faith.

- As leaders, it can be difficult to trust God at times, to surrender control to Him and to leave the results in His capable hands.

NOTES

LEADERSHIP REBORN

2. FEARFUL OF NO HEIR

- As Abram was waiting on the Lord's timing, he began to get fearful.

- He was afraid that the blessings that the Lord promised would mean little since he had no sons of his own.

- However, God promised Abram he would have a son of his own.

THE WORD

- *"You have given me no descendants of my own, so one of my servants will be my heir.' Then the LORD said to him, 'No, your servant will not be your heir, for you will have a son of your own who will be your heir.'" (Genesis 15:3-4, NLT)*

- **Go Deeper:** Genesis 15:1-6

THE POINT

- Abram's faith prevailed over his fear. He trusted God to provide a son for him even though he was old.

- His belief and trust in the Lord proved his faith was genuine.

- Sometimes fear keeps us from the things God has for us. Do you ever get fearful that God won't come through?

- Leading well calls us to push through and hold onto our faith despite our fears.

NOTES

_____

_____

_____

_____

_____

LEADERSHIP REBORN

3. FORCEFUL OF HIS OWN PLAN

- Life is full of waiting. Waiting tests our patience and our faith.
- God's waiting room can be a lonely and difficult place. Do you ever get tired of waiting on God?
- Abram and Sarai got tired of waiting. About ten years went by and they still did not have a son. So, they decided to make their own plan.

THE WORD

- *"So after Abram had been living in Canaan ten years, Sarai his wife took her Egyptian slave Hagar and gave her to her husband to be his wife. He slept with Hagar, and she conceived."* *(Genesis 16:3-4, NIV)*
- **Go Deeper:** Genesis 16:1-4, 16:15-16

THE POINT

- Abram and Sarai took matters into their own hands. As a result, rivalry and tension formed between Hagar and Sarai and later between their offspring.
- Abram tried to force things, but that is not what God intended. God intended to bless Abram and his wife with their own child.
- The temptation to go off on our own is strong. However, leading well requires patient endurance to wait on the Lord and His timing.

NOTES

LEADERSHIP REBORN

4. FORGETFUL OF GOD'S PROMISES

- People are forgetful at times, and that can be costly when it comes to our faith. Forgetting God's promises is a sure way to derail our faith.

- In the waiting and in the fear, Abram forgot. He forgot God's promises and questioned if he was really going to have a true heir.

- Abram left his homeland when he was 75. After 24 years, at the age of 99, the Lord reminded him of his covenant promise.

THE WORD

- *"…Then God said to him, 'This is my covenant with you: I will make you the father of a multitude of nations! What's more, I am changing your name. It will no longer be Abram. Instead, you will be called Abraham, for you will be the father of many nations.'" (Genesis 17:3b–5, NLT)*

- *"Abraham was 100 years old when Isaac was born." (Genesis 21:5, NLT)*

- **Go Deeper:** Genesis 17:1-8

THE POINT

- As a sign of God's covenant and future blessing, He changed Abram's name to Abraham and Sarai's name to Sarah.

- God promised Abraham that his wife would have a son. God was faithful. Indeed, a year later Isaac was born.

- Faith-based leaders must find ways to remember God's promises and remind themselves and the people they lead that God is ever faithful.

NOTES

LEADERSHIP REBORN

5. FREEDOM OF LETTING GO

- It is not easy to let go. The struggle for control is powerful, and our leadership instincts don't give up control very often.

- Abraham's struggle for control of his life was real, but he slowly learned to trust the Lord's plans. After 25 years, Abraham finally had a son, Isaac.

- There is a rare freedom in giving up control to God who knows all, sees all, and understands all things.

THE WORD

- *"Take your son, your only son—yes, Isaac, whom you love so much—and go to the land of Moriah. Go and sacrifice him as a burnt offering on one of the mountains, which I will show you." (Genesis 22:2, NLT)*

- **Go Deeper:** Genesis 22:1-2, 22:12-14

THE POINT

- After Isaac grew up a bit, the Lord asked even more of Abraham… the ultimate surrender of control. He asked Abraham to sacrifice his son.

- Crazy! Why would God bless Abraham with a son only to take him away?

- It was an extremely difficult test of Abraham's faith, and a test of God's provision.

- Amazingly, Abraham obeyed and trusted that God would provide.

- He released his grip of control and surrendered to God's power. He did things God's way, and he was rewarded.

NOTES

LEADERSHIP REBORN

THE CHANGE

- How does infusing faith into our leadership affect how we view and handle power?

- Faith releases control and changes our view and use of power in three ways.

1. Surrender control to God and lean on His wisdom and guidance.
2. God is in charge, and we answer to Him regardless of our role or position.

3. Leading well means handling power wisely and sharing it with others.

THE SPOTLIGHT: COMPANY CONFLICTS

- What do these companies have in common: Facebook, Twitter, Google, Apple, Etsy, Volkswagen, L'Oréal, and Disney?

- They each have had significant power struggles within their company's top leadership. Power struggles often reveal an ugly side of leadership.

- Disney changed CEOs in 2020, but the results were less than ideal.

- Conflict grew between the current and former CEO and trickled down creating frustration among employees. It left workers wondering 'Who's in charge?'

- All these companies have struggled to handle their success and their leadership well. Thankfully, we can learn from their mistakes and forge a better path.

THE APPLICATION: PUTTING IT INTO PRACTICE

- Reflect, discuss, and apply the following questions as they relate to your leadership within your company, team, church, school, or family.

1. What are some of the power struggles you have faced in your life and leadership?

2. Why is power so dangerous, and how can you share it and manage it wisely?

3. How can you invite God into your leadership, acknowledge His power, and release control to Him?

4. How does infusing faith into your leadership affect how you view and handle power?

5. In what ways can you relate to Abraham's difficulty in waiting on God, his fear of not being in control, or his trying to force his own plan?

6. Seeking God's will for our lives isn't easy. How do we know which paths to take and which ones to avoid?

MY BIG TAKEAWAYS

1.

2.

3.

LEADERSHIP REBORN

SESSION 7
CHANGE IN PERSPECTIVE

KEY QUESTION: What Matters Most?

FEATURED LEADER: Joseph

STORY: Microscopes vs. Telescopes

- Microscopes help us study things that are very small and have totally changed our perspective of cell biology, medicine, and disease.

- Telescopes help us see things very far away and have totally changed our perspective of the stars, planets, and the universe.

- Both devices offer us a unique perspective that is beyond our normal vision, and each perspective can help us see life differently.

- Often in life, we can lose perspective and struggle to see and understand things in the proper light.

OVERVIEW

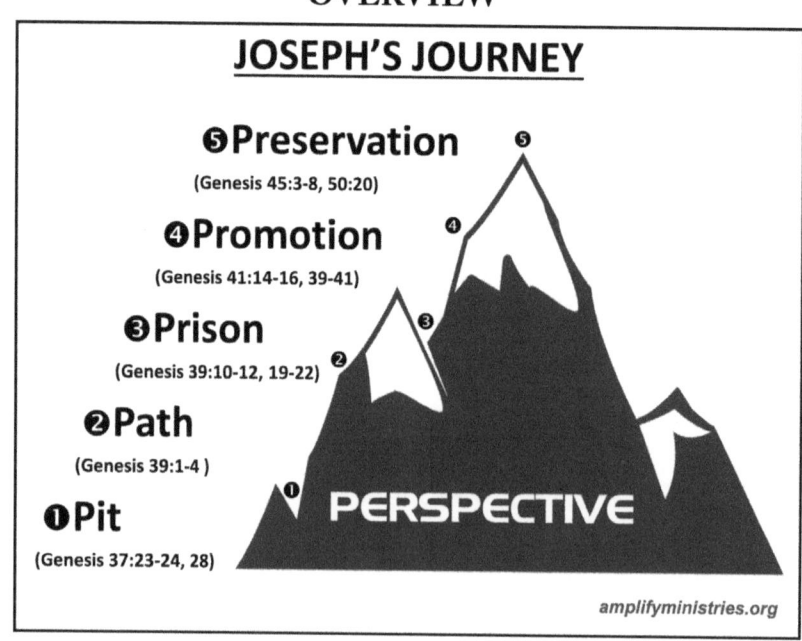

1. PIT OF BETRAYAL

- Joseph didn't have an easy life. His journey was filled with blessing and betrayal, success and slavery, joy and jail time, prosperity and pain.
- Between their dad's favoritism and Joseph's dreams, his ten older brothers became jealous and began to hate him.
- Joseph's brothers plotted against him and planned to kill him. So, at the age of seventeen, Joseph found himself at the bottom of a pit.

THE WORD

- *"So when Joseph arrived, his brothers ripped off the beautiful robe he was wearing. Then they grabbed him and threw him into the cistern. Now the cistern was empty; there was no water in it." (Genesis 37:23-24, NLT)*
- **Go Deeper:** Genesis 37:25-28

THE POINT

- Betrayed by his brothers and nearly left for dead, Joseph was then sold into slavery by his brothers instead and exiled to another country.
- Betrayal cuts deep and the pain can linger a long time making it difficult to move forward. Questions fill our minds: Why did this happen to me? Does God care?
- Joseph's life completely shifted, as he became a teenage slave in a foreign land.
- Eventually, Joseph would have to deal with his brothers' betrayal, but for now, Joseph held on to his faith and survived.
- Joseph's journey was one of those times when perspective was elusive.

NOTES

LEADERSHIP REBORN

2. PATH TO EGYPT

- Joseph was taken to Egypt as a slave and re-sold to the captain of Pharaoh's guard where he was made a house servant.

- Even in slavery, God was with him.

- Despite being a slave and being exiled from his family, Joseph made the best of a bad situation. He worked hard and relied on the Lord.

THE WORD

- *"When Joseph was taken to Egypt by the Ishmaelite traders, he was purchased by Potiphar, an Egyptian officer. Potiphar was captain of the guard for Pharaoh, the king of Egypt." (Genesis 39:1, NLT)*

- **Go Deeper:** Genesis 39:1-4

THE POINT

- Joseph's perseverance and resilience were remarkable.

- He gained the favor of his master and was rewarded with a rare leadership position. He was placed in charge of his master's whole house.

- Joseph's ability to keep moving forward, to press on, and to work hard despite his circumstances was a testimony to his faith and to God's blessing on him.

NOTES

LEADERSHIP REBORN

3. PRISON OF THE FORGOTTEN

- As time went on, Joseph caught the attention of Potiphar's wife. She found him attractive and tried many times to seduce him.
- He turned down her advances and kept his distance. Despite his honorable character, Joseph was falsely accused of taking advantage of her.
- In her scorn, Potiphar's wife framed Joseph and lied about what happened.

THE WORD

- *"Potiphar was furious when he heard his wife's story about how Joseph had treated her. So he took Joseph and threw him into the prison where the king's prisoners were held, and there he remained."* (Genesis 39:19-20, NLT)
- **Go Deeper:** Genesis 39:10-12, 39:21-22

THE POINT

- Joseph went to jail for a crime he did not commit. Falsely accused. Falsely imprisoned. Joseph lost his position, and his life took another downturn.
- Betrayed again, he was left in prison for years and was eventually forgotten.
- Remarkably, Joseph earned the favor and trust of the prison warden and was placed in charge of the other prisoners. Even in jail, he had a leadership role.
- Joseph had very little perspective on what God was doing in his life and why. His limited view from prison, slavery, and the well made it hard to see clearly.
- Joseph's journey reminds us that leading well requires no small amount of perseverance and faith, especially in the absence of perspective.

NOTES

LEADERSHIP REBORN

4. PROMOTION BY PHARAOH

- Years went by, and the Pharaoh of Egypt began having some disturbing dreams that his advisors could not interpret or understand.

- Upon hearing from one of his attendants that Joseph could interpret dreams, Pharaoh summoned Joseph from jail.

- Joseph interpreted Pharaoh's dreams to mean that seven years of plenty were coming followed by seven years of famine in the land.

THE WORD

- *"Then Pharaoh said to Joseph, 'Since God has revealed the meaning of the dreams to you, clearly no one else is as intelligent or wise as you are. You will be in charge of my court, and all my people will take orders from you. Only I, sitting on my throne, will have a rank higher than yours.' Pharaoh said to Joseph, 'I hereby put you in charge of the entire land of Egypt.'" (Genesis 41:39–41, NLT)*

- **Go Deeper:** Genesis 41:14-16

THE POINT

- Pharaoh was impressed with Joseph and his wisdom from God. As a result, He promoted Joseph to be second in command of all of Egypt.

- Pharaoh realized that there was no one better than Joseph to provide leadership over the coming famine.

- Joseph began to see why God had him sent to Egypt and started to see the bigger picture. In that moment, he got a glimpse of perspective.

- Leading well challenges us to be faithful in the small things regardless of our vantage point and trust that God sees the big picture even when we can't.

NOTES

LEADERSHIP REBORN

5. PRESERVATION OF THE PEOPLE

- As the seven years of plenty began, Joseph collected and stored grain to distribute to the people later during the coming famine.
- The famine struck hard and severely crippled the surrounding regions with starvation and death.
- Joseph's relief efforts in Egypt became the central hub for foreign aid to the entire population, including Canaan where his family lived.
- Joseph's father sent his brothers to Egypt to buy food. Upon their arrival, the brothers came face to face with Joseph but did not recognize him.

THE WORD

- *"Take You intended to harm me, but God intended it all for good. He brought me to this position so I could save the lives of many people." (Genesis 50:20, NLT)*
- **Go Deeper:** Genesis 45:3-8

THE POINT

- Joseph recognized his brothers but kept his identity hidden to test them.
- He had one brother imprisoned, provided provisions for the others, and demanded they return with their youngest brother to prove their loyalty.
- After over twenty years, Joseph was reunited with his brothers. He invited them into the palace and revealed his true identity to them.
- Finally, Joseph gained perspective. He could see that God had a plan to use his life to preserve the lives of all the people, including his own family.
- Even though we may not see it or understand it, God has a plan, and He is an expert at redeeming what was lost.

NOTES

LEADERSHIP REBORN

THE CHANGE

- How does infusing faith into our leadership affect our perspective and the lens through which we view things?

- Faith renews our perspective and what's important in three key ways.

1. Holding on to our faith matters most and gives us perspective.
2. God is present and at work even in our darkest times, and deepest pain.
3. Look for the bigger picture and consider what God may be doing.

THE SPOTLIGHT: ABRAHAM LINCOLN

- Abraham Lincoln lost many political races and faced a lot of rejection and adversity before he became the President of the United States.

- One of the reasons he was able to move from failure to success can be attributed to his faith and reliance on God.

- One of the biggest challenges that Lincoln faced during his presidency was the issue of slavery and fighting for the rights of others.

- Neither Lincoln nor Joseph knew how God would use them to change the course of history and how their leadership would make a huge difference.

THE APPLICATION: PUTTING IT INTO PRACTICE

- Reflect, discuss, and apply the following questions as they relate to your leadership within your company, team, church, school, or family.

1. What are some experiences in your life that have given you perspective?

_____

_____

2. How has God been present and at work even in your darkest times, deepest pain, and hardest difficulties?

_____

_____

3. Pause for a moment and ask God to give you a renewed sense of perspective about your life, your circumstances, and your leadership.

_____

_____

4. How does infusing faith into your leadership affect your perspective on things?

_____

_____

5. In what ways can you relate to Joseph's journey of being in the pit or prison, of not having perspective, of struggling to forgive, or of finding victory?

_____

_____

MY BIG TAKEAWAYS

1. _____

2. _____

3. _____

LEADERSHIP REBORN

SESSION 8
CHANGE IN OUTCOMES

KEY QUESTION: How Do You Succeed?
FEATURED LEADER: Paul

STORY: Olympic Snowboarding

- Shaun White is a U.S. Olympic gold medalist and X-Games snowboarding champion who has faced his share of adversity.

- At the 2014 Winter Olympics, he was seriously injured during a complicated trick when he landed wrong on the rim of the half-pipe.

- One of his secrets to successfully overcoming adversity and mounting a major comeback was developing mental toughness.

- Sometimes, the right mentality makes all the difference.

OVERVIEW

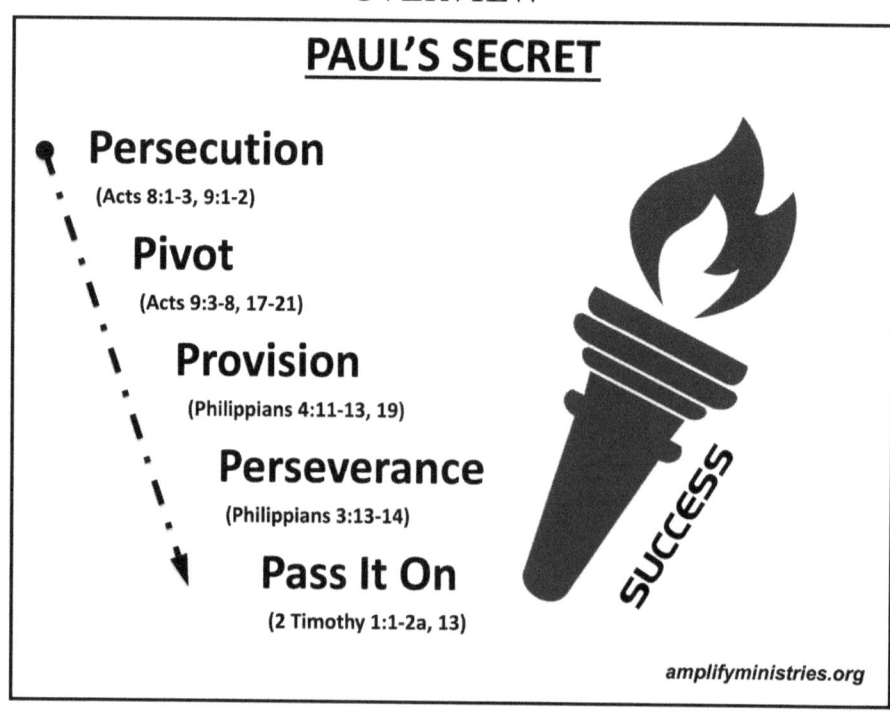

1. PERSECUTION OF BELIEVERS

- We have a choice about how we use our leadership abilities. We can use them for good or for bad purposes.
- Saul was against the teachings of Jesus and was attacking the Christian church by killing its followers or putting them in prison.
- Saul had great influence and was responsible for a massive outbreak of persecution against the followers of Christ. As a result, people feared him.

THE WORD

- *"But Saul was going everywhere to destroy the church. He went from house to house, dragging out both men and women to throw them into prison." (Acts 8:3, NLT)*
- **Go Deeper:** Acts 8:1-3, 9:1-2

THE POINT

- Saul became notorious for his actions and the followers of Jesus grew deeply concerned for their own safety.
- In Saul's zeal to protect the Jewish law and teachings, the Christian church suffered.
- Saul had become a powerful leader, but he was not leading well.
- Violence and oppression are not the answer. There is a better way to lead.

NOTES

LEADERSHIP REBORN

2. PIVOT TOWARD GOD

- Saul was about to have an experience with God that would change his life, his leadership, and his faith forever.

- Because Saul had been persecuting the church and its followers so harshly, he gained the attention of Jesus himself.

- As Saul was traveling, the Jesus he didn't believe in appeared to him suddenly and interrupted his trip in a dramatic and powerful way.

- Jesus wanted Saul to stop persecuting the church and decided to make a memorable impression on him.

THE WORD

- *"He fell to the ground and heard a voice saying to him, "Saul! Saul! Why are you persecuting me?" "Who are you, lord?" Saul asked. And the voice replied, "I am Jesus, the one you are persecuting!"* (Acts 9:4-5, NLT)

- **Go Deeper:** Acts 9:3-8, 9:17-21

THE POINT

- Saul's encounter with Jesus changed his life. He pivoted 180 degrees in his thinking and in his faith and changed allegiances.

- Transformed by the power of Christ, Saul started preaching and using his leadership abilities to build up the church instead of trying to destroy it.

- Saul the persecutor went on to become Paul the missionary; he was truly a changed man.

- Paul's transformation shows us the power of a changed life. It's amazing what can happen when God gets a hold of our lives and our leadership.

NOTES

LEADERSHIP REBORN

3. PROVISION TO LEAN ON

- Paul's change came at great personal cost as he would learn through his sufferings to lean on Christ for His provision.
- Paul was shipwrecked, put on trial, imprisoned, beaten, and suffered greatly for the cause of Christ.
- Through it all, he learned an amazing life lesson that would become the secret to Paul's success.

THE WORD

- *"For I can do everything through Christ, who gives me strength." (Philippians 4:13, NLT)*
- **Go Deeper:** Philippians 4:11-13, 4:19, 3:7-8

THE POINT

- Paul's mantra became "I can do everything through Christ." That was the secret to his success, and it has become a rally cry for many people of faith today.
- Paul believed it, and he lived it. Through thick and thin, good and bad, joy and pain, Christ was all he needed.
- In many ways, this redefined success for him, and it redefines success for us. It is not about recognition or reward; it's about being faithful to God first.
- Faith-based leadership looks at success through the lens of faithfulness. Were you faithful to God?

BONUS: In my leadership context as a student pastor, we defined the key to great teamwork as S.U.C.C.E.S.S. Maybe this acronym will help you too.

- **S acrifice:** work hard and give above and beyond
- **U nity:** promote harmony and avoid division
- **C ooperation:** work together and follow instructions
- **C ommunication:** listen well, speak clearly, and respond often
- **E ncouragement:** support and build up your teammates
- **S elflessness:** put the team and your teammates first
- **S ignificance:** champion the cause and show value to others

NOTES

LEADERSHIP REBORN

4. PERSEVERANCE TO PRESS ON

- As Paul left his old way of life behind and pursued his new life in Christ, he was persecuted for it.

- Ironically, some of the same opposition that he was responsible for creating now became an obstacle for him.

- As he took the message of God into the religious, political, and philosophical arenas of Athens, Rome, Ephesus, and Corinth, Paul persevered.

THE WORD

- *"...But one thing I do: Forgetting what is behind and straining toward what is ahead, I press on toward the goal to win the prize for which God has called me heavenward in Christ Jesus."* *(Philippians 3:13-14, NIV)*

- **Go Deeper:** Romans 5:3-5, 1 Corinthians 9:24-27

THE POINT

- In the face of opposition and persecution, Paul pressed on. As a result, churches began to grow, and the message of the Gospel spread throughout the region.

- Paul's perseverance and determination were an inspiration to the early church, and he became a champion of their faith.

- Like Paul, we must hold fast to our faith, train hard, persevere, and run to win.

- In life, in faith, and in leadership, we must press on with a resilient and forged determination.

NOTES

LEADERSHIP REBORN

5. PASS IT ON

- It's hard to win a relay race if you don't pass the baton to the next runner. The hand-off is critical.

- Many races are won or lost based on a team's ability to execute good hand-offs between runners. Leadership is the same way.

- Paul wasn't satisfied with being a good leader himself. He knew the importance of passing on his faith and his leadership to others.

THE WORD

- *"I am writing to Timothy, my dear son.... Hold on to the pattern of wholesome teaching you learned from me—a pattern shaped by the faith and love that you have in Christ Jesus."* *(2 Timothy 1:2a, 13, NLT)*

- **Go Deeper:** 2 Timothy 1:1-2, 1 Corinthians 9:19-22

THE POINT

- Paul invested in the younger generation of leaders and pastors through his teaching, letters, and visits. Specifically, he invested a lot in Timothy.

- Leading well means taking the time to train others to lead well and to pass on the torch of leadership to those around us.

- In training others to lead well, we multiply our leadership, increase our impact, and help future leaders succeed.

NOTES

LEADERSHIP REBORN

THE CHANGE

- How does infusing faith into our leadership affect how we view and handle success?

- Faith redefines success and how we view outcomes in three key ways.

1. We pivot our leadership toward God and are faithful to Him first.
2. Faith-based leaders rely on Christ for the strength to lead well.

3. Successful leaders persevere and pass on their leadership and their faith.

THE SPOTLIGHT: THE WRIGHT BROTHERS

- The Wright brothers designed and tested many wing and airplane designs but were unable to achieve the necessary lift and control for sustained flight.

- The key to their eventual success was a pivot in their thinking and designs.

- The Wright brothers' work redefined successful aviation design and flight mechanics for all those who would follow in their footsteps.

- Like building an airplane, leading well takes practice, repetition, experimentation, perseverance, pivoting at times, and passing on our knowledge and skills.

THE APPLICATION: PUTTING IT INTO PRACTICE

- Reflect, discuss, and apply the following questions as they relate to your leadership within your company, team, church, school, or family.

1. How could your leadership pivot more toward God and away from other things?

_____

_____

2. What would it take to redefine success as faithfulness to God first and to other goals second?

_____

_____

3. How can you pass on your leadership and faith to others?

_____

_____

4. How does infusing faith into your leadership affect how you view and handle success?

_____

_____

5. How have you had to persevere in your leadership, and how has God provided for you along the way?

_____

_____

MY BIG TAKEAWAYS

1. _____

2. _____

3. _____

LEADERSHIP REBORN

SESSION 9
CHANGE IN CREDIT

KEY QUESTION: Who Gets the Glory?
FEATURED LEADER: Moses

STORY: The Watergate Scandal

- Leadership can be a tricky thing. If handled poorly, bad decisions and questionable choices can quickly spiral into scandal and corruption.

- One of the most infamous leadership and political scandals in the United States was Watergate involving Republican leaders spying on the Democrats.

- As White House counsel to Richard Nixon, John Dean was one of the primary players in the Watergate scandal and the complex cover-up that followed.

- The quest for personal glory is a dangerous road. Our own ego and desire for fame and fortune can blind us and sabotage our leadership.

OVERVIEW

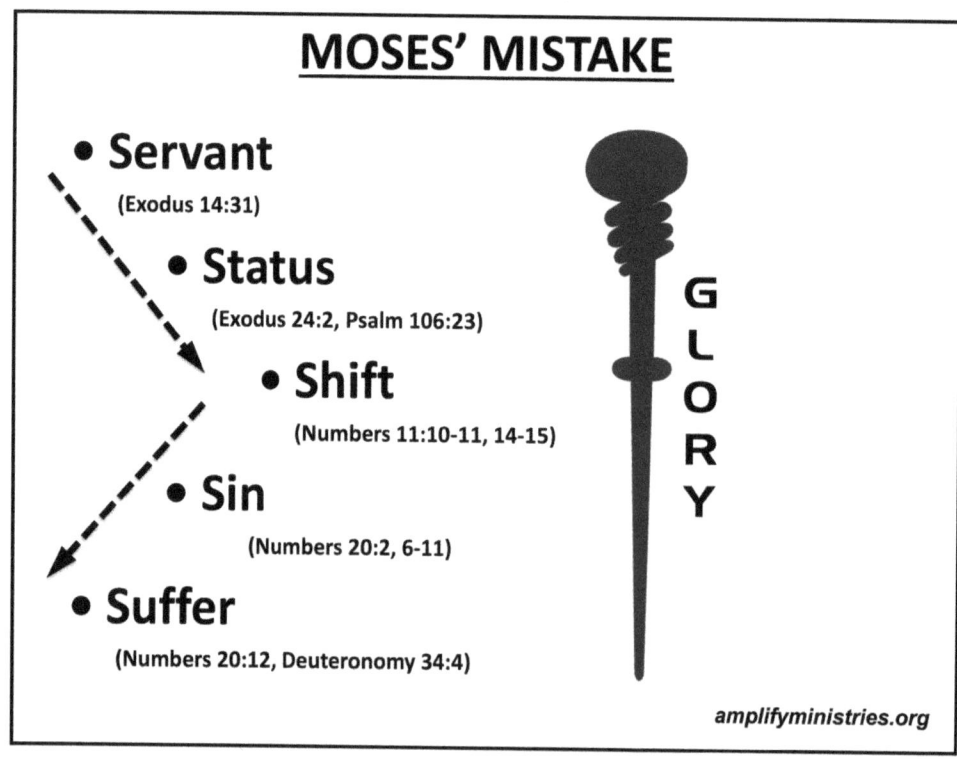

1. SERVANT OF THE LORD

- Moses was a Hebrew born in captivity and raised in Egypt.
- After fleeing from Egypt as an adult, he was called by God to go back and free his people, the Israelites, from slavery.
- Moses was a reluctant leader, but he eventually agreed to serve the Lord and lead the people out of Egypt.

THE WORD

- *"When the people of Israel saw the mighty power that the LORD had unleashed against the Egyptians, they were filled with awe before him. They put their faith in the LORD and in his servant Moses." (Exodus 14:31, NLT)*
- **Go Deeper:** Exodus 14:5-31

THE POINT

- After God used Moses to part the Red Sea and help the Israelites escape from Pharaoh's armies, the people trusted Moses to lead them as God's servant.
- By helping free the people of Israel from slavery in Egypt, Moses had earned the people's respect.
- Sometimes leadership must be earned. It takes time to build trust with the people we are leading, especially in a new role.

NOTES

LEADERSHIP REBORN

2. STATUS AS GOD'S CHOSEN MEDIATOR

- Moses was God's chosen representative to act as a mediator between God and the people of Israel.

- Moses had a special role and connection with God that at times gained him status with the people and at other times made the people afraid of him.

- As mediator, Moses bore the responsibility of communicating God's instructions to the people, intervening on their behalf, and helping them follow God.

THE WORD

- *"… But Moses, his chosen one, stepped between the LORD and the people. He begged him to turn from his anger and not destroy them. (Psalm 106:23b, NLT)*

- **Go Deeper:** Exodus 24:2, 34:29-30, 1 Timothy 2:5

THE POINT

- Being God's chosen mediator was a heavy responsibility and a dangerous one.

- At times, Moses had to step in when the people messed up and begged God for their very lives.

- Israel was God's chosen people, but they lacked wisdom and needed a leader to guide them, an advocate to plead for them, and accountability to follow God.

NOTES

_____

_____

_____

_____

_____

LEADERSHIP REBORN

3. SHIFT IN THINKING

- As a leader, do you ever get tired of the people you are leading? Do the people you lead, supervise, train, and develop ever get on your nerves?
- It is not easy leading people. Do you ever get tired of their complaining, their repeated mistakes, and their short-sightedness?
- Leading others can be frustrating at times, and Moses was feeling many of those frustrations in a big way.

THE WORD

- *"Moses heard all the families standing in the doorways of their tents whining, and the LORD became extremely angry. Moses was also very aggravated." (Numbers 11:10, NLT)*
- **Go Deeper:** Exodus 32:19-20, Numbers 11:10-11, 11:14-15, 14:1-2

THE POINT

- Moses' frustration with the people of Israel grew as they complained about the food, the wandering in the desert, and his leadership.
- Their complaining was so aggravating and ridiculous that God got angry, Moses wanted to die, and the people wished they were back in Egypt.
- What happens when the shepherd gets sick and tired of leading the stubborn and stinky sheep? Moses' thinking shifted inward, and it opened the door for sin.

NOTES

LEADERSHIP REBORN

4. SIN CREEPS IN

- The people of Israel rebelled against Moses because there was no water to drink. Again, Moses took the blame and his frustration continued to mount.
- They had forgotten how God provided water for them before and were complaining once more.
- God gave Moses very specific instructions to follow and planned to miraculously provide the people with water from a rock.
- Instead of speaking to the rock like God instructed him to do, Moses struck the rock with his staff.

THE WORD

- *"Then Moses raised his hand and struck the rock twice with the staff, and water gushed out. So the entire community and their livestock drank their fill." (Numbers 20:11, NLT)*
- **Go Deeper:** Numbers 20:2, 20:6-11, Exodus 17:5-6

THE POINT

- In striking the rock, Moses took credit for the miracle that God did. Out of frustration with the people, he elevated himself and took the glory.
- Moses decided to flex his power in front of the people; the power that God had given him. He took the honor intended for God.
- In doing so, he sinned and committed a huge leadership mistake; a mistake for which he was later punished.
- If we don't handle the frustrations of leadership wisely, they will grow within us, leaving us open to critical mistakes and sinful actions.
- In our work as leaders, we must continually give God the glory.

NOTES

_____

_____

_____

_____

_____

LEADERSHIP REBORN

5. SUFFER THE CONSEQUENCES

- Sin has consequences. Moses had to pay the price for disobeying God, and the price was heavy.

- Because he took credit for God's miracle, Moses was not allowed to enter the Promised Land which he had been waiting a long time to do.

- Not being allowed to enter the land was a tough consequence. In some ways, it may even seem unfair.

THE WORD

- *"But the LORD said to Moses and Aaron, "Because you did not trust in me enough to honor me as holy in the sight of the Israelites, you will not bring this community into the land I give them." (Numbers 20:12, NIV)*

- **Go Deeper:** Deuteronomy 34:1-7

THE POINT

- To soften the blow, God showed Moses an act of kindness and allowed him to see the land from a mountain top.

- The honor of taking the people into the Promised Land was given to Joshua instead.

- Leaders aren't perfect. We make mistakes from time to time, but it can be hard to face the consequences of our actions.

- Leading well requires us to own our mistakes, and work hard to avoid them in the first place by taking steps to address our weaknesses.

NOTES

LEADERSHIP REBORN

THE CHANGE

- How does infusing faith into our leadership affect how credit is given?
- Faith redistributes the credit and who gets the glory in three key ways.

1. Give God the glory in all things.
2. Leading well means having a humble heart and surrendering your pride.
3. Share the credit, elevate your team, and help others succeed.

THE SPOTLIGHT: THE RISE AND FALL OF VEGGIETALES®

- VeggieTales® and Big Idea Productions started as a company that made animated kids' videos about Bible stories using talking vegetables.
- The founder, Phil Vischer, spoke at a conference about the rise and fall of his company.
- His company became very popular and grew rapidly, until his dream fell apart as internal division rose, pride surfaced, and sales declined.
- There is a danger in our leadership journey of crossing the line and shifting our focus from building God's kingdom to building our own.
- To lead well, we need to continually give God the glory and keep our eyes fixed on Him.

SECTION SUMMARY

Great job finishing up the eight fundamentals that change when we infuse our leadership with faith. Coming up next, we'll discuss the enemies to faith-based leadership and how we can overcome them.

THE APPLICATION: PUTTING IT INTO PRACTICE

- Reflect, discuss, and apply the following questions as they relate to your leadership within your company, team, church, school, or family.

1. What does it look like to give God the glory and share the credit with the people you lead?

_____

_____

2. Describe a time when your pride got in the way of leading well. How could a humbler approach have been helpful?

_____

_____

3. How do you handle things when the people you lead frustrate you and don't want to follow you?

_____

_____

4. How does infusing faith into your leadership affect how credit is given?

_____

_____

5. Have you ever had success and been tempted to take the credit and the glory for yourself, to brag, to boast, to show off, or to think too highly of yourself? Explain.

_____

_____

> **MY BIG TAKEAWAYS**
> 1. _____
> 2. _____
> 3. _____
>
> LEADERSHIP REBORN

SESSION 10
THE ENEMY OF OUR FAITH

KEY QUESTION: Who's Our Enemy?
FEATURED LEADER: Satan

BACKGROUND:

- Understanding your opponent's tactics and strategies can help you come up with an effective battle plan.

- In the battle of good versus evil, God is on one side and Satan is on the other.

- Satan is a leader. He's not a good one, but an incredibly effective one; villains often are. He is smart, organized, strategic, crafty, powerful, and dangerous.

- His power and reach are limited, and his fate has already been decided. Until then, we must do battle against the forces of darkness.

"For our struggle is not against flesh and blood, but against the rulers, against the authorities, against the powers of this dark world and against the spiritual forces of evil in the heavenly realms." (Ephesians 6:12, NIV)

OVERVIEW

SATAN'S DECEPTION

- **Deceiving the World**
  o (Revelation 12:7-9)

- **Distorting the Truth**
  o (John 8:44)

- **Delivering Temptation**
  o (Matthew 4:1, 1 Thessalonians 3:5)

- **Developing Darkness**
  o (Ephesians 2:2, 2 Corinthians 4:4)

- **Destroying Humanity**
  o (Revelation 9:11, 12:17, 1 Peter 5:8)

SIN

amplifyministries.org

1. DECEIVING THE WORLD

- Have you ever watched a movie with a plot twist? At a critical point in the story, it is revealed that one of the characters has been deceiving people.

- Can you recall any classic movie deceptions and betrayals?

- In reality, there is a deception currently going on in the world and Satan is the one trying to deceive all of us.

THE WORD

- *"But This great dragon—the ancient serpent called the devil, or Satan, the one deceiving the whole world—was thrown down to the earth with all his angels." (Revelation 12:9, NLT)*

- **Go Deeper:** Revelation 12:7-9, 12:12

THE POINT

- Satan is perhaps running the biggest scam and deception of all time.

- He deceives people into believing God doesn't exist, doesn't care, or isn't worth following. Satan wants us to doubt, question, and abandon our faith.

- He also deceives people into believing that he isn't real or isn't a threat. Be careful in your thinking, so that you are not deceived by the enemy.

- Faith-based leaders learn to recognize the enemy's deceptions and expose his lies.

NOTES

LEADERSHIP REBORN

2. DISTORTING THE TRUTH

- Satan is a master at deception and an expert at lying. That's part of what makes him a formidable enemy.

- He has a sneaky way of making wrong things seem right and right things seem wrong.

- He is also really good at underselling the consequences and getting us to believe that our sinful actions, thoughts, and choices aren't that big of a deal.

THE WORD

- *"When he lies, he speaks his native language, for he is a liar and the father of lies."* *(John 8:44b, NIV)*

- **Go Deeper:** John 8:44a, Genesis 3:1-7, 3:13-15

THE POINT

- Satan has been a liar from the beginning. From lying and deceiving Adam and Eve to distorting the truth while tempting Jesus.

- He whispers lies to us, tempts us to believe wrong things about ourselves, and distorts our perception.

- He tempts us to question God and doubt the Bible, twists the truth, and tries to convince us to abandon our faith

- Don't fall for his tricks. Hold on to the truth of God's Word, expose the lies for what they are, and keep living and leading with honor.

NOTES

LEADERSHIP REBORN

3. DELIVERING TEMPTATION

- Temptations come in many forms. Satan and his forces are great at dressing up sin in all kinds of appealing ways.
- The enemy plays on our appetites, knows our weaknesses, and offers up a poison apple at just the right time.
- The enemy often waits until just the right moment to attack. He tempted Jesus when he was tired, hungry, and alone.

THE WORD

- *"Then Jesus was led by the Spirit into the wilderness to be tempted there by the devil." (Matthew 4:1, NLT)*
- **Go Deeper:** 1 Thessalonians 3:5, 1 Corinthians 10:12-13, Matthew 6:13

THE POINT

- The temptation to lie, cheat, steal, lust, drink, curse, or take drugs can be addictive and hard to stop.
- Even the best leaders can struggle with temptations of all kinds.
- All of the biblical leaders we have discussed faced temptations. Some gave in and some stood firm in their faith.
- David was tempted, gave in, and committed adultery. Joseph was tempted, stood firm, and ran from sin.
- The temptations we face are powerful, but they can be overcome.
- Faith-based leaders learn to recognize the enemy's tactics and take steps to protect themselves and their leadership from temptations.
- Leading well means resisting the temptations we face, asking trusted friends to hold us accountable, and seeking forgiveness when we make mistakes.

NOTES

LEADERSHIP REBORN

4. DEVELOPING DARKNESS

- When you were young, were you afraid of the dark?

- Our enemy and his tactics thrive in darkness. The forces of darkness are called that for a reason.

- Satan's forces are really good at covert operations and developing darkness within us. They oppose the light and actively try to avoid being exposed.

- Sin grows in the dark and thrives in secret.

THE WORD

- *"You used to live in sin, just like the rest of the world, obeying the devil—the commander of the powers in the unseen world. He is the spirit at work in the hearts of those who refuse to obey God."* *(Ephesians 2:2, NLT)*

- **Go Deeper:** 2 Corinthians 4:4

THE POINT

- One of the enemy's tactics is to keep us isolated and in the dark, struggling in secret and all alone.

- The more we give in to sin, the more the darkness and shame grow within us, and the more disconnected from God we become.

- Faith-based leadership fights the darkness and resists the drift to the dark side.

- Leading well means living in the light and shining the light of God's Word on the dark areas of our lives.

- Faith-based leaders push back the darkness with the light of Christ and seek to help others out of the darkness.

NOTES

LEADERSHIP REBORN

5. DESTROYING HUMANITY

- War often causes destruction. Destroyed cities, destroyed armies, and devastated countries are the result of many hard-fought battles.

- Most people don't realize that there is an unseen war raging on in our world. There is a spiritual battle going on for the hearts and lives of people.

- Satan, the Destroyer, actively opposes the people, plans, and purposes of God.

- He wants to destroy our lives, our leadership, and our loyalty to God.

THE WORD

- *"Their king is the angel from the bottomless pit; his name in Hebrew is Abaddon, and in Greek, Apollyon—the Destroyer." (Revelation 9:11, NLT)*

- *"Put on all of God's armor so that you will be able to stand firm against all strategies of the devil." (Ephesians 6:11, NLT)*

- **Go Deeper:** Revelation 12:17, 1 Peter 5:8

THE POINT

- How do we combat such an enemy bent on our destruction?

- Thankfully, Jesus Christ is our champion, the Holy Spirit gives us power, and the Father has a plan. In addition, God gives us spiritual armor to protect us.

- The Bible is our weapon, faith is our shield, prayer is our provision, and the forces of light are fighting on our behalf.

- Faith-based leaders need to be on guard, alert, self-controlled, clothed in God's armor, courageous, righteous, full of love, wise, and steadfast in their faith.

NOTES

LEADERSHIP REBORN

THE SPOTLIGHT: AN INSIDE LOOK

- Most followers of God, especially those in leadership and ministry, can share stories about the spiritual opposition they have experienced.

- When we try to lead well, live right, and serve the Lord, there is opposition.

- We have experienced strong spiritual opposition in many ways ranging from:
  - Personal struggles, Health issues
  - Kids acting out, Stuff breaking down
  - Marriage conflicts, Family drama
  - Job difficulties, Work conflicts
  - Financial problems, Trouble sleeping
  - Communication issues, Fierce opposition
  - Blocked goals, Unanswered prayers

- While many of these things are common, we would argue that the timing, cause, frequency, intensity, and destructive effects were the result of spiritual attacks.

- These issues aren't always spiritual opposition, but sometimes they are.

THE RUB: Spiritual Opposition

- How does infusing faith into our leadership affect how we view and handle opposition?

- Faith redefines the battlefield and helps us identify the real enemy.

1. Consider how the enemy tries to attack your leadership and character.
2. Consider how the enemy influences the people you lead and tries to disrupt your team's effectiveness.
3. Discern the difference between traditional obstacles and spiritual opposition. Then take steps to address them.

CLOSING THOUGHTS

- We realize that sessions on Satan and the spiritual opposition to our leadership can be disturbing, a bit scary, and depressing. However, that's not the intent.
- The goal is to help prepare you as a leader for the battles you may face and to identify our seldom talked about and rarely understood enemy.

THE APPLICATION: PUTTING IT INTO PRACTICE

- Reflect, discuss, and apply the following questions as they relate to your leadership within your company, team, church, school, or family.

1. In what ways have you faced spiritual opposition in your faith journey and in your leadership roles?

_____

_____

2. **Look Inward:** What personal temptations might be disrupting your leadership?

_____

_____

3. **Look Outward:** What destructive forces or behaviors might be disrupting your organization, team, or family?

_____

_____

4. **Be Discerning:** What steps do you need to take to evaluate and address the traditional obstacles and spiritual opposition to your leadership?

_____

_____

5. How does the harsh reality of a spiritual enemy affect how you lead?

_____

_____

MY BIG TAKEAWAYS

1. _____

2. _____

3. _____

LEADERSHIP REBORN

SESSION 11
THE ENEMY'S DOMAIN

FOCUS: The World
FEATURED LEADER: Satan

- There are insightful leadership principles that we can learn from how Satan has influenced our environment and culture.

- Over time, we can be fooled into building our lives on the wrong foundation.

- As a result, we end up thinking the wrong things; we focus on the wrong things; we want the wrong things; and we chase the wrong things.

OVERVIEW

SATAN'S DOMAIN

- **Worldly Culture**
  - ○ **Wrong Foundation** (Matthew 7:24-27)

- **Worldly Values**
  - ○ **Wrong Thinking** (Romans 1:28-32, 12:2)

- **Worldly Focus**
  - ○ **Wrong Priorities** (Matthew 16:26, 6:33)

- **Worldly Motives**
  - ○ **Wrong Intentions** (James 4:2-4)

- **Worldly Pace**
  - ○ **Wrong Speed** (Exodus 20:8-10a, Psalm 46:10)

WORLD

amplifyministries.org

1. WORLDLY CULTURE: WRONG FOUNDATION

THE STORY

- In construction, building a strong and level foundation is critical. The whole project depends on it; just ask the builders of the Leaning Tower of Pisa.
- This crooked tower in Italy serves as an embarrassing reminder of how important it is to have a good foundation.
- While the ancient marble tower continues to be a site for tourism, its unstable foundation has made it infamous and unsafe.

THE CONNECTION

- Similarly, Satan has helped shape our culture in such a way that many people's lives are crooked and have been built on the wrong foundation.
- Does the current culture of the world promote the things of God?
- Popular culture tends to promote: instant gratification, consumerism, wealth, pleasure, escape, entitlement, and selfishness.
- Our society has lost its moral center and has twisted things upside down and backward.

THE WORD

- *"Therefore everyone who hears these words of mine and puts them into practice is like a wise man who built his house on the rock." (Matthew 7:24, NIV)*
- **Go Deeper:** Matthew 7:24-27

THE POINT

- How do you build your life on a strong foundation?
- Leading well means building our lives on the firm foundation of God's Word and putting His principles into practice in our daily lives.
- Faith-based leaders resist the urge to build their lives on the shifting sands of the culture.

NOTES

LEADERSHIP REBORN

2. WORLDLY VALUES: WRONG THINKING

THE STORY

- Have you ever been told you did something wrong?
- When I was in first grade the teacher told me I did the coloring assignment wrong. I thought I did it right, but my thinking was incorrect.

THE CONNECTION

- Similarly, many people don't realize that their thinking is wrong, and they have been chasing the wrong things.
- Popularity, status, power, beauty, fashion, achievement, possessions, and money don't last and don't satisfy the longings in our hearts.
- Often, our identity gets wrapped up in these things. When it fades away, we are left empty.

THE WORD

- *"Since they thought it foolish to acknowledge God, he abandoned them to their foolish thinking and let them do things that should never be done. Their lives became full of every kind of wickedness, sin, greed, hate, envy, murder, quarreling, deception, malicious behavior, and gossip." (Romans 1:28-29, NLT)*
- **Go Deeper:** Romans 1:28-32, 12:2

THE POINT

- The enemy has sold us the wrong values and most people have believed it.
- As a result, people have come to value the wrong things and think the wrong things about their lives and their pursuits.
- When we pursue worldly values and embrace wrong thinking, it breeds corrupt behavior.
- Leading well challenges worldly thinking and points us toward godly living.

NOTES

_____

_____

_____

_____

_____

LEADERSHIP REBORN

3. WORLDLY FOCUS: WRONG PRIORITIES

- Do you ever struggle with how to prioritize your time?
- The enemy wants us to focus on the wrong priorities and distract us into spending our time in an exhausting pursuit of the wrong stuff.
- If we are not careful, we can quickly start skipping or bailing on things that are vital to our health and longevity.
- Satan loves when we trade the vital and eternal things for the temporary.

THE WORD

- *"And what do you benefit if you gain the whole world but lose your own soul? Is anything worth more than your soul?" (Matthew 16:26, NLT)*
- **Go Deeper:** Matthew 6:33, 22:36-40, Galatians 5:19-21, Hebrews 12:1b-2a

THE POINT

- We all struggle to spend our lives and our time wisely. Many people get their priorities flipped and shifted out of order.
- Problems usually arise when we focus on the wrong things and don't make the most important things a priority first.
- What wrong priorities do you see in our world?
- If you are looking for some help in prioritizing your life, here's a checklist for what order to pursue things based on Scripture and my personal opinion.

1. **Love God:** First
   - Reach Up: to know and love God
   - Reach In: to grow and mature in faith

2. **Love People:** Second
   - Reach Out: to serve and love others
     - 2nd Love Your Spouse (if married)
     - 3rd Love Your Kids (if it applies)
     - 4th Love Others (serve, be a light, make disciples)
     - 5th Work/School/Chores/Responsibilities
     - 6th Sports/Clubs/Hobbies/Recreation/Entertainment

(Fill in the chart by listing how/where you spend your time and evaluating if things need to change)

MY CURRENT PRIORITIES	MY IDEAL PRIORITIES
1.	1.
2.	2.
3.	3.
4.	4.
5.	5.
6.	6.
7.	7.
8.	8.

4. WORLDLY MOTIVES: WRONG INTENTIONS

- If we were to shine a light on your motives, what would we find?
- Hopefully, you are an honest person with honorable motives. However, it might depend on the circumstances or the topic at hand.
- Motives and intentions are internal matters of the heart that are not easily seen, discerned, or revealed.
- The enemy is really good at twisting our desires. If he can't get us to do the wrong things, he tries to get us to do the right things with the wrong motives.

THE WORD

- *"...Yet you don't have what you want because you don't ask God for it. And even when you ask, you don't get it because your motives are all wrong—you want only what will give you pleasure."* (James 4:2b-3, NLT)
- **Go Deeper:** James 4:1-4, Ephesians 5:10-13

THE POINT

- There is no shortage of selfish motives in the world and misguided intentions.
- Leading with the wrong intentions can be a dangerous thing. It leaves our leadership open to manipulation and conflicting agendas.
- Leading well means asking God to search our hearts and purify our motives and intentions.
- Faith-based leaders seek to surrender their selfish motives to God and ask Him to help them lead with honorable intentions.

NOTES

LEADERSHIP REBORN

5. WORLDLY PACE: WRONG SPEED

THE STORY

- Most fans of NASCAR and IndyCar racing are familiar with the purpose of a pace car. While the pace car is out front, it regulates everyone's speed.
- Also, long-distance runners must pace themselves to spread out their energy and speed throughout the race so that they don't peak too soon.
- Finding the right running pace can be tricky and takes practice: too fast and you burn out, too slow and you won't win.

THE CONNECTION

- Similarly, pace also plays a key role in our lives and our leadership. What is your current life pace? How busy are you? How stressed are you?
- Most of the world operates at a fast pace. Some cultures have a slower pace, but overall our world functions at lightning speed.
- Most of us don't have much margin, buffer, rest, or renewal in our lives.

THE WORD

- *"You have six days each week for your ordinary work, but the seventh day is a Sabbath day of rest dedicated to the LORD your God." (Exodus 20:9-10a, NLT)*
- **Go Deeper:** Exodus 20:8-11, Psalm 46:10, Matthew 11:28-30

THE POINT

- The enemy loves to distract us by keeping us so busy and by keeping the pace so high that we don't take time for what's most important.
- We end up being evaluated on our productivity (how much), efficiency (how fast), and accuracy (how correct) we can do things without regard for our health.
- Setting a healthy pace for yourself and those you lead is critical.
- Slow down and take some time to evaluate what a healthy pace looks like for your leadership context and re-adjust your pace.

NOTES

LEADERSHIP REBORN

THE SPOTLIGHT: STRESS

- Stress is a part of life and can be beneficial, but also harmful.
- **Beneficial:** stress can help us to better ourselves and rise to the challenge.
- **Harmful:** stress can distract us and hurt our body when our pace gets hectic.

STRESS RESPONSE

- In a typical stress response, many systems turn on and prepare for fight/flight.
- If it's a matter of survival, our body increases energy supply, muscle strength, brain activity, heart rate, and blood pressure to respond to a threat.
- The problem is that most daily stress situations are not life-threatening.
- As a result, the repeated intensity of our triggered stress response can wear down the body causing us to feel fatigue, exhaustion, and run down.

HARMFUL EFFECTS

- Some of the harmful effects of prolonged stress include: high blood pressure, heart disease, heart attack, mental health issues, emotional distress, weight gain, and trouble sleeping.

COPING MECHANISMS

- **Poor Coping:** alcohol, drugs, tobacco, over/under eating, self-harm, self-indulgence, and addictive behaviors only mask our problems.
- **Better Coping:** exercise, healthy diet, journaling, talking to friends, praying, listening to music, sharing with a counselor, or slowing the pace.

PAUSE

- Take a moment to breathe and find comfort in these words from Jesus:
- *"Then Jesus said, 'Come to me, all of you who are weary and carry heavy burdens, and I will give you rest.'" (Matthew 11:28, NLT)*
- The pressure and pace of life weigh heavily on all of us.
- Leading well means slowing the hustle of life to take inventory of our current pace and re-adjust our speed.

THE RUB: Leading in an Uncooperative World

- How does infusing faith into our leadership affect our view of the environment in which we lead?
- Faith reevaluates our leadership landscape as we seek to lead others in a fallen world in three key ways.

1. We need to combat the enemy's influence on lives and leadership.
2. Recognize how the worldly environment and culture affect the people we lead.
3. We learn to counter the cultural norms with faith-based alternatives.

THE APPLICATION: PUTTING IT INTO PRACTICE

- Reflect, discuss, and apply the following questions as they relate to your leadership within your company, team, church, school, or family.

1. **Look Inward:** How has the enemy influenced your foundation, thinking, priorities, motives, and pace?

_____

_____

2. **Look Outward:** How is the current worldly culture affecting your company, team, church, school, or family?

_____

_____

3. **Become Counter-cultural:** What cultural norms do you and your group need to counter with faith-based alternatives?

_____

_____

4. How does infusing faith into your leadership affect your view of the environment in which you lead?

_____

_____

5. What happens when people have the wrong foundation, thinking, priorities, motives, and pace?

_____

_____

MY BIG TAKEAWAYS

1. _____

2. _____

3. _____

LEADERSHIP REBORN

SESSION 12
THE ENEMY WITHIN

KEY QUESTION: Why Am I Corrupt?
FEATURED LEADER: Adam

- Many people don't realize that there is a hidden enemy deep within us that corrupts our lives and our leadership.

- There is an ugly selfishness that hides beneath the surface and taints our motives, drives our hearts, shapes our thinking, and twists our behavior.

- We don't like to admit it, but in our honest moments alone with our hearts, we know there is something off and deeply wrong inside of us.

OVERVIEW

ADAM'S CURSE

- **Choices and Consequences**
  (Genesis 2:15-17, 3:6, Galatians 6:7-8)
- **Corrupt Nature**
  (Romans 5:12, 18-19)
- **Corrupt Heart**
  (Mark 7:21-23, Jeremiah 17:9)
- **Corrupt Mind**
  (Romans 8:5-8)
- **Corrupt Behavior**
  (Galatians 5:19-21)

CORRUPTION

amplifyministries.org

1. CHOICES AND CONSEQUENCES

- Life is full of choices: fun choices, tough choices, good choices, bad choices, and everything in between.
- Each choice we make has positive or negative consequences. Some are mild, and some have a heavy impact.
- Adam was the father of humanity. He was given free will, guidelines, and the ability to make his own choices, and so was his wife, Eve.
- As the first humans, God created them this way and gave them freedom to make their own decisions.
- As representatives of the entire human race, Adam and Eve's choices had a massive impact on all the people to come.

THE WORD

- *"But the LORD God warned him, "You may freely eat the fruit of every tree in the garden— except the tree of the knowledge of good and evil. If you eat its fruit, you are sure to die."* (Genesis 2:16-17, NLT)
- **Go Deeper:** Genesis 3:6, Galatians 6:7-8

THE POINT

- Adam chose poorly. Adam and Eve gave into temptation, ate the forbidden fruit, and broke God's command.
- Their sin marked the fall of humanity, and the consequences of their choices would ripple throughout history. Humankind was never the same after that.
- Our nature would be forever changed and humanity's right relationship with God was now broken.

NOTES

LEADERSHIP REBORN

2. CORRUPT NATURE

- Adam disobeyed God and sin entered the world.
- As a result, Adam and Eve were cursed, banished from the Garden of Eden, and a sinful nature was passed on to all of humanity.
- From them, the corruption spread to all of us, and we all bear the curse as well.

THE WORD

- *"When Adam sinned, sin entered the world. Adam's sin brought death, so death spread to everyone, for everyone sinned."* (Romans 5:12, NLT)
- **Go Deeper:** Romans 5:18-19

THE POINT

- What does it mean that we all have a sinful or corrupt nature?
- It means that sin has corrupted God's original design for us. The corruption of sin penetrates all aspects of our being: heart, mind, and behavior.
- Think of it this way… sin is a lot like salt. Salt is corrosive to metal just like sin is corrosive to our lives.
- Our sinful nature is the enemy within us, and it undermines our leadership.
- Leading well means that each of us must battle against sin and corruption within ourselves.

NOTES

LEADERSHIP REBORN

3. CORRUPT HEART

- From a corrupt nature comes a corrupt heart.
- Corruption can be found almost anywhere: politics, businesses, judicial systems, police departments, churches, and athletic competitions.
- It is vital to protect ourselves and our leadership from corruption. We must identify our weaknesses and be alert.

THE WORD

- *"For from within, out of a person's heart, come evil thoughts, sexual immorality, theft, murder, adultery, greed, wickedness, deceit, lustful desires, envy, slander, pride, and foolishness. All these vile things come from within; they are what defile you." (Mark 7:21–23, NLT)*
- **Go Deeper:** Jeremiah 17:9, James 1:14-15

THE POINT

- The enemy within us seeks to destroy our leadership, ruin our credibility, and sabotage our relationships.
- Leading well requires a careful evaluation of our own hearts and sinful desires and takes steps to guard against the temptations we face.
- It is a daily challenge to keep our sinful natures and corrupt hearts in check.

NOTES

LEADERSHIP REBORN

4. CORRUPT MIND

- A corrupt heart leads to a corrupt mind.

- We all wrestle with corrupt thoughts from time to time. It is easy to allow our minds to wander and end up thinking some pretty wild thoughts.

- With so many things trying to influence us, it can be a real struggle to push the noise aside and hold on to what's right and true.

- The real struggle for our mind is not external, but internal. The real battle is inside our heads.

THE WORD

- *"Those who are dominated by the sinful nature think about sinful things, but those who are controlled by the Holy Spirit think about things that please the Spirit. So letting your sinful nature control your mind leads to death. But letting the Spirit control your mind leads to life and peace."* (Romans 8:5-6, NLT)

- **Go Deeper:** Romans 8:5-8, 12:2

THE POINT

- Leading well means taking action against our corrupt thoughts, feeding our minds biblical truth, and anchoring our thinking in sound teaching and principles.

- It takes a disciplined and renewed mind to lead well.

- Faith-based leadership recognizes our corrupt minds and engages in the daily battle to renew our thinking, and to purify our minds.

NOTES

LEADERSHIP REBORN

5. CORRUPT BEHAVIOR

- Our corrupt nature spreads to our hearts, minds, and behavior.
- We are all broken people, and we act badly at times.
- In a moment of frustration, it can be easy to lash out in some unholy ways.
- It is common to yell and scream, cuss and swear, punch and kick, or to mock and insult people who offend and annoy us.

THE WORD

- *"When you follow the desires of your sinful nature, the results are very clear: sexual immorality, impurity, lustful pleasures, idolatry, sorcery, hostility, quarreling, jealousy, outbursts of anger, selfish ambition..." (Galatians 5:19-20a, NLT)*
- **Go Deeper:** Galatians 5:19-23, Romans 7:18-21

THE POINT

- It's not pretty, but sinful people sin. We do stupid, mean, and selfish stuff.
- We sin, mess up, hurt people, act inappropriately, and our behavior can be downright nasty and unacceptable.
- While our corrupt behavior is just a symptom of a corrupt heart and mind, it's the ugliest and messiest part of our corruption because it's what people see.
- Faith-based leaders fight the urge to behave badly and seek to honor God and others with their actions.
- Leading well means acting well, and that takes a lifetime of self-control, personal discipline, lots of apologies, making better choices, and a resilient faith.

NOTES

LEADERSHIP REBORN

THE RUB: The Inner Battle

- How does infusing faith into our leadership affect how we view the nature of people?

- Faith identifies a hidden enemy within us and highlights the inner battle that we all must face.

The Enemy Within Us: Leading Ourselves

- It's a leadership fact, leaders are flawed. Even the best leaders have flaws, shortcomings, and weaknesses.

- Leading well means admitting our flaws and taking steps to address our corrupt nature.

The Enemy Within Them: Leading Fallen People

- It's a leadership fact, people are flawed. We lead in a world full of flawed, corrupted, and fallen people.

- Recognizing that the people we are leading have a corrupt nature will help us have a stronger sense of compassion and understanding toward them.

- To lead well, we must battle the enemy within ourselves and learn how to deal with the enemy within other people.

THE SPOTLIGHT: THE REALITY OF LEADING

- People will be late to meetings, drop the ball, miss the goal, forget the report, offend the client, talk behind our backs, break promises, and disappoint us.

- Because of that, leading fallen people requires a generous amount of love, care, and forgiveness.

- People can also hit the mark, win the game, make sacrifices, overcome, rise above, strengthen the team, and come through for us in big ways.

- It takes a proper balance of leadership, inspiration, correction, understanding, and support.

Remember, the people and teams you lead are only human, so try not to let corrupt behavior surprise you. Sinful people sin. You don't have to accept it but expect it from time to time. They are on a journey just like you. Offer correction; give guidance; and forgive often. Challenge them to be better; lead by example; and love them regardless.

THE APPLICATION: PUTTING IT INTO PRACTICE

- Reflect, discuss, and apply the following questions as they relate to your leadership within your company, team, church, school, or family.

1. How does having to battle with your own fallen nature affect how you lead?

2. How does having to deal with other people's fallen nature affect how you lead them?

3. What can you do to guard your life and your leadership from sin and corruption?

4. How does infusing faith into your leadership affect how you view the nature of people?

5. What roles do compassion, grace, forgiveness, and correction play in leading corrupt people in a corrupt world?

MY BIG TAKEAWAYS

1.

2.

3.

LEADERSHIP REBORN

SESSION 13
VICTORY OVER THE ENEMY

KEY QUESTION: How Can I Win?
FEATURED LEADER: You

OVERVIEW

OUR VICTORY

❶ **Surrender to God**
(Psalm 51: 1-4a, 1 John 1:8-9)

❷ **Start Trusting**
(Proverbs 3:5-6, Psalm 25:4-5)

❸ **Stop Sinning**
(Colossians 3:5-10)

❹ **Stand Firm**
(1 Corinthians 16:13-14, 1 Peter 5:8-9)

❺ **Seek Accountability**
(Galatians 6:1-2)

F A I T H

amplifyministries.org

THE STORY

- Usually, the road to recovery starts with admitting you need help.

- If you are familiar with addiction and recovery groups it might go something like this: *"My name is Larry, and I am a sinful person."*

- The group applauds: "Welcome to the Sinful Person Recovery Group! You have taken the first step on the road to a better life and better leadership."

- Overcoming the corruption within us and leading a life of victory begins with an honest look inside ourselves and a willingness to surrender.

1. SURRENDER TO GOD

What do we do about our corrupt nature?

- The solution to a corrupt nature is a new nature.
- The solution to a corrupt heart is a spiritual heart transplant.
- The solution to a corrupt mind is a renewed mind.
- The solution to corrupt behavior is a completely transformed life.
- None of these things can be done on our own.

THE WORD

- *"Wash me clean from my guilt. Purify me from my sin. For I recognize my rebellion; it haunts me day and night." (Psalm 51:2-3, NLT)*
- **Go Deeper:** Psalm 51:1-4, 1 John 1:8-9

THE POINT

- God is the only one who can help us, and it starts with surrendering our hearts, minds, and lives to Him.
- While the first step in fighting a corrupt nature is our initial confession of sins and surrender of our lives to Christ. There is also an ongoing component.
- Faith-based leadership continually surrenders our hearts, minds, and behaviors to God and asks him to forgive us, purify us, and protect us.

THE PRAYER: Leadership Prayer of Surrender

"Jesus, help me lead well today. I surrender my life and my leadership to you. Forgive my sinfulness and purify my motives and desires. Help me serve, love, and value the people I am leading. Bless my leadership and may it honor you. Please, protect me from all the enemies of my leadership both inside of me and outside of me. Grant me victory in the name of Jesus. Amen."

NOTES

LEADERSHIP REBORN

2. START TRUSTING

- Having victory over the enemy of our faith and the enemy within us involves trusting ourselves less and trusting God more.

- Faith-based leaders don't just trust God occasionally; they live lives that are regularly dependent on Him.

- It is vital to our leadership that we continually trust and rely on God.

THE WORD

- *"Trust in the LORD with all your heart; do not depend on your own understanding. Seek his will in all you do, and he will show you which path to take." (Proverbs 3:5–6, NLT)*

- **Go Deeper**: Psalm 25:4-5

THE POINT

- Asking God for help and guidance becomes a lifelong habit and empowers us to lead well.

- Develop a teachable spirit and be open to what God is trying to accomplish in you and through you.

THE PRAYER: Leadership Prayer of Trust

"God, I put my trust in you today. Help me lead well by relying on your wisdom and direction. I recognize the limits of my own wisdom and understanding, and I seek your guidance. I leave all my plans and decisions up to you. Show me which paths to take. Please, lead me as I lead others, and bless my leadership. In the name of Jesus, I pray. Amen."

NOTES

_____

_____

_____

_____

_____

LEADERSHIP REBORN

3. STOP SINNING

- Having victory over the enemies of our leadership takes hard work, perseverance, and self-control.
- Spiritual growth is a life-long journey, and we are all at different places along the path.
- It is hard to lead well if we are living in sin.

THE WORD

- *"So put to death the sinful, earthly things lurking within you…"* (Colossians 3:5, NLT)
- *"Put on your new nature and be renewed as you learn to know your Creator and become like him."* (Colossians 3:10, NLT)
- **Go Deeper**: Colossians 3:5-10, Galatians 5:24-25

THE POINT

- Recognizing our poor thoughts and behaviors, confessing them to God, and then turning away from them is an essential part of having personal victory.
- The goal is to sin less and to become more and more like Christ in our attitudes, thoughts, and actions.
- Stopping the sin in our lives and choosing to live for God is a daily struggle and a lifelong process. We constantly need Christ's help to do it.
- Leading well means striving to live honorably and sin less but leaning hard on God's grace and forgiveness when we make mistakes.

THE PRAYER: Leadership Prayer of Confession

"Jesus, help me stop sinning and lead a life that honors you. I confess that I think and act in ways that are sinful and dishonorable. Please, forgive me for my mistakes and help me live better. Bless my leadership and help me lead well by resisting temptation and choosing to avoid sinful things. Purify my heart, mind, body, and actions, and help me become more like you. I pray in your name. Amen."

NOTES

LEADERSHIP REBORN

4. STAND FIRM

- Like a lighthouse stands firm as a guardian of light and protects ships, our faith can help us stand firm and protect our leadership from danger.
- Leadership is dangerous and faith-based leadership is especially dangerous because the Enemy does not want us to lead well.
- Faith-based leaders are under ongoing spiritual attack and must learn to stand firm against the forces of darkness.

THE WORD

- *"Be on guard. Stand firm in the faith. Be courageous. Be strong. And do everything with love."* *(1 Corinthians 16:13-14, NLT)*
- *"Therefore, put on every piece of God's armor so you will be able to resist the enemy in the time of evil. Then after the battle you will still be standing firm." (Ephesians 6:13, NLT)*
- **Go Deeper**: 1 Peter 5:8-9, James 4:7-8

THE POINT

- The forces of darkness and light are real. Whether we recognize them or not, we feel their effects on us all the time.
- It can be difficult to stand firm in the face of challenging circumstances. Be on guard, hold up the shield of your faith, stand your ground, and resist the enemy.
- Life can quickly become stressful, overwhelming, and hard to handle. Therefore, it is essential to draw near to God, and clothe ourselves in His armor.

THE PRAYER: Leadership Prayer of Strength

"Lord, help me stand firm in my faith and cling to the hope I have in you. Please give me the strength and endurance that I need to lead well today. I come near to you and resist the enemy. Help me be strong and courageous and give me a steady heart to face whatever the day holds. Help me be a light for you and for the people I lead. I pray in the name of Jesus. Amen."

```
NOTES




```

LEADERSHIP REBORN

5. SEEK ACCOUNTABILITY

- It is not easy to live a life of faith and to lead well on your own.

- It takes good people in your life who care about your health and well-being to help you keep your life, faith, and leadership on track.

THE WORD

- *"Dear brothers and sisters, if another believer is overcome by some sin, you who are godly should gently and humbly help that person back onto the right path." (Galatians 6:1a, NLT)*

- **Go Deeper**: Proverbs 27:17, Galatians 6:1-2, Ecclesiastes 4:9-10

THE POINT

- Inviting trusted friends to hold you accountable to high standards of conduct and faith can make a big difference and keep you in leadership for a long time.

- Personally, my close friends have played a vital role in my leadership journey.

- I encourage you to find and build some accountability into your life and take a risk by opening up with some trusted people to better yourself.

THE PRAYER: Leadership Prayer of Accountability

"God, help me seek accountability in my life. Please provide trusted friends to help me follow you and lead well. Bring the right people into my life to help strengthen my faith, help me resist sin, and become a better person. Help me be honest about my struggles, confess when I make mistakes, and set goals to improve myself. Help me lead well today by keeping my life and heart on the right path. In Jesus name, Amen."

NOTES

LEADERSHIP REBORN

THE WIN: Personal Victory

- How does infusing faith into our leadership affect how we pursue victory in our personal lives?

- Faith redefines our ability to overcome and gives us a new set of tools to achieve personal victory.

- By surrendering to God, trusting Him, resisting sin, standing firm, and seeking accountability, we can have victory over the enemies to our leadership.

- Through our faith we can address the problem of corruption within our own hearts, tackle it with the power of God, and find victory over the darkness.

- While the struggle to lead well is ongoing, it is possible to live a life of victory and lead victoriously.

THE PRAYER: Leadership Prayer of Victory

"Jesus, give me victory over the sin in my life and over my sinful nature. Protect me from the power and influence of Satan and help me stand firm in my faith. Help me lead well today by surrendering to you, trusting your leading in my life, and being accountable to my close friends. Please, grant me personal victory over the darkness and help me lead victoriously. I pray in your name. Amen."

THE APPLICATION: PUTTING IT INTO PRACTICE

- Reflect, discuss, and apply the following questions as they relate to your leadership within your company, team, church, school, or family.

1. How does gaining victory in your personal life affect your leadership?

2. What are some steps you can take to resist a specific sin, to stand firm in your faith, and to ask a friend to help keep you on track?

3. If you haven't yet, take some time to pray the various leadership prayers. Which leadership prayer impacted you the most and why?

4. How does infusing faith into our leadership affect how we pursue victory in our personal lives?

5. How has your faith in God helped you have personal victory in your life?

MY BIG TAKEAWAYS

1.

2.

3.

LEADERSHIP REBORN

SESSION 14
THE ART OF LEADING WELL

ALLOWING YOUR FAITH TO INFUSE YOUR LEADERSHIP

- This entire video course and study guide are dedicated to the art of leading well. Let's review the main principles, key questions, featured leaders, and the changes that faith-based leadership challenges us to make.

THE PURPOSE: Course Review

1. To help you remember what we have covered
2. To help you break the material down into smaller manageable parts
3. To help you pick areas to focus on

THE BIG PICTURE

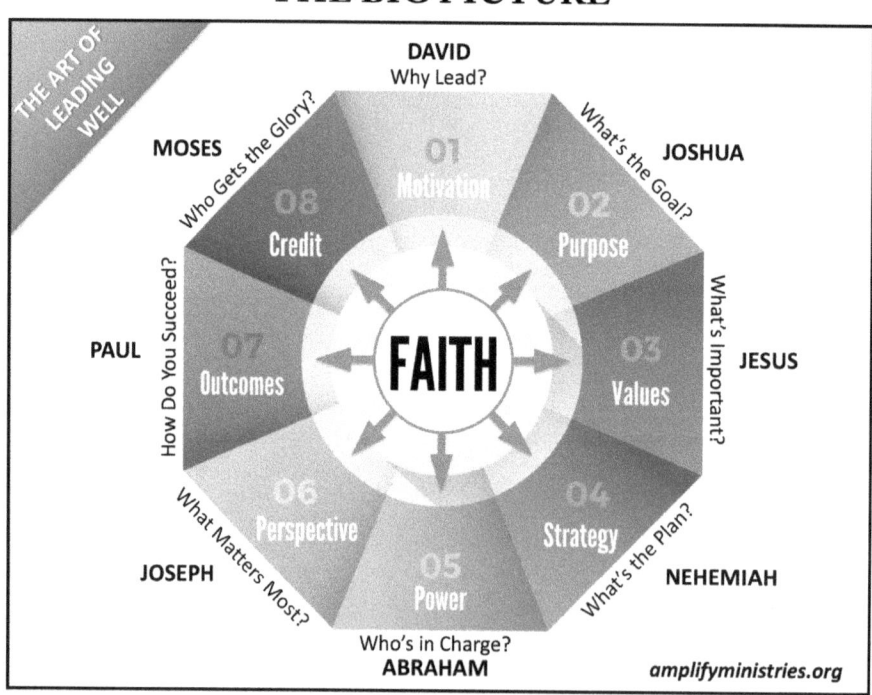

- When our faith is at the center of our leadership, it fuels our motivation, purpose, values, and strategy, and it shapes our view of power, perspective, outcomes, and credit.

1. LEADING WELL

- The world is full of leaders, and a lot of people can lead, but not everyone leads well. Actually, most people don't lead well.
- Leading well is an art.
- It is a combination of learned leadership skills, natural talent, hard work, experience, God-given ability, personal development, and allowing your faith to infuse all aspects of how you lead.
- The art of leading well requires more than traditional leadership models and skills, it requires faith in God.
- Faith makes our leadership better.

You can lead well, and your leadership can be REBORN with faith at the center.

2. CHANGE IN MOTIVATION: Why Lead?

From David's leadership and his heart for God, we learned:
- How he was **called** to lead
- How he was **committed** to God
- How he was **challenged** to give up
- How he was **confirmed** as king
- How he was **contrite** and open-hearted

How does faith change our motivation? Faith *reframes* our motivation, why we lead, and how we motivate others in three key ways.
1. Leading well starts with the leader's heart.
2. Our faith adds a spiritual aspect to why we lead.
3. Faith changes how we motivate others.

3. CHANGE IN PURPOSE: What's the Goal?

From Joshua's leadership and the way he led the people of Israel, we learned about:
- A **cause** to believe in
- His **courage** to lead
- His **character** to honor God
- His **conviction** to follow through
- The **covenant** he renews

How does faith change our purpose? Faith *refocuses* our purpose and the goal of our leadership in three key ways.
1. Spiritual Life: Love God and honor him above all.
2. Private Life: Strong inner character and integrity protect our effectiveness.
3. Community Life: Caring for the hearts, souls, and lives of others.

4. CHANGE IN VALUES: What's Important?

From Jesus' leadership and the way He valued people, we learned about:
- How He was **sent** by God
- His **service** to others
- His **sacrifice** for others
- How He provides **salvation** for all
- How He provides **support** for His followers

How does faith change our values? Faith *reprioritizes* our values and what's important in three key ways.
1. Leading well requires biblical values at its core.
2. The value of people is paramount. Value people over profits, programs, and procedures.
3. Leadership at its base level is rooted in building healthy relationships.

5. CHANGE IN STRATEGY: What's the Plan?

From Nehemiah's leadership and his strategy to rebuild Jerusalem, we learned how:
- He **prayed** often
- He **planned** well
- He **provided** for his workers
- He **protected** his people
- He **prevailed** over opposition

How does faith change our strategy? Faith *reforms* our strategy and how we accomplish the plan in three key ways.
1. Our strategy must fit with the values and purposes of the Bible.
2. Invite God into the strategy development process.
3. Share the plan, delegate jobs, and release your team to do it.

6. CHANGE IN POWER: Who's in Charge?

From Abraham's leadership and the way he struggled for control, we learned:
- He was **faithful** to follow God
- He was **fearful** of no heir
- He was **forceful** of his own plan
- He was **forgetful** of God's promises
- He found **freedom** in letting go

How does faith change our view of power? Faith *releases* control and changes our view and use of power in three key ways.
1. Surrender control to God and lean on His wisdom and guidance.
2. God is in charge, and we answer to Him regardless of our role or position.

3. Leading well means handling power wisely and sharing it with others.

7. CHANGE IN PERSPECTIVE: What Matters Most?

From Joseph's leadership and his struggle to gain perspective, we learned about
- The **pit** of betrayal
- His **path** to Egypt
- The **prison** of the forgotten
- His **promotion** by Pharaoh
- The **preservation** of the people

How does faith change our perspective? Faith *renews* our perspective and what's most important in three key ways.
1. Holding on to our faith matters most and gives us perspective.
2. God is present and at work even in our darkest times, and deepest pain.
3. Look for the bigger picture and consider what God may be doing.

8. CHANGE IN OUTCOMES: How Do You Succeed?

From Paul's leadership and the way he viewed success, we learned about:
- His **persecution** of believers
- How he **pivots** toward God
- His **provision** to lean on God
- His **perseverance** to press on
- His desire to **pass** on his leadership

How does faith change our view of outcomes? Faith *redefines* success and how we view outcomes in three key ways.
1. We pivot our leadership toward God and are faithful to Him first.
2. Faith-based leaders rely on Christ for the strength to lead well.
3. Successful leaders persevere and pass on their leadership and their faith.

9. CHANGE IN CREDIT: Who Gets the Glory?

From Moses' leadership and the mistakes he made along the way, we learned about:
- His role as a **servant** of the Lord
- His **status** as God's chosen mediator
- His **shift** in thinking
- How **sin** crept into his heart
- How he **suffered** the consequences

How does faith change our view of credit? Faith *redistributes* the credit and who gets the glory in three key ways.
1. Give God the glory in all things.

2. Leading well means having a humble heart and surrendering your pride.

3. Share the credit, elevate your team, and help others succeed.

10. THE ENEMY OF OUR FAITH: WHO'S OUR ENEMY?

From the tactics and strategies of Satan's leadership, we learned about him:
- **Deceiving** the world
- **Distorting** the truth
- **Delivering** temptation
- **Developing** darkness
- His goal of **destroying** humanity

How does faith change our view of opposition? Faith *redefines* the battlefield and helps us identify the real enemy in three key ways.

1. Consider how the enemy tries to attack your leadership and character.
2. Consider how the enemy influences the people you lead.
3. Discern the difference between traditional obstacles and spiritual opposition. Then take steps to address them.

11. THE ENEMY'S DOMAIN: WHERE'S OUR ENEMY?

From how Satan has shaped the worldly environment we live in, we learned how he has distorted things through:
- Our **worldly culture**
- Society's **worldly values**
- People's **worldly focus**
- Individual's **worldly motives**
- Our collective **worldly pace**

How does faith change our view of the environment in which we lead? Faith *reevaluates* our leadership landscape as we seek to lead others in a fallen world in three key ways.

1. We need to combat the enemy's influence on lives and leadership.
2. Recognize how the worldly environment and culture affect the people we lead.
3. We learn to counter the cultural norms with faith-based alternatives.

12. THE ENEMY WITHIN: WHY AM I CORRUPT?

From Adam's leadership and how his corrupt nature was passed along to us, we learned about:
- His **choices and consequences**
- Our **corrupt nature**
- Our **corrupt hearts**
- Our **corrupt minds**
- Our **corrupt behavior**

How does faith change our view of the nature of people? Faith *reveals* a hidden enemy within us and highlights the inner battle that we all face.

The Enemy Within Us: Leading Ourselves

1. It's a leadership fact, leaders are flawed, and we need to admit our flaws.
2. Leading well means taking steps to address our corrupt nature.

The Enemy Within Others: Leading Fallen People

1. It's a leadership fact, people are flawed. We lead fallen people.
2. Recognizing that the people we are leading have a corrupt nature will help us have a stronger sense of compassion and understanding toward them.

13. VICTORY OVER THE ENEMY: HOW CAN I WIN?

From choosing to live a life of faith and developing our own leadership, we learned to have victory over the enemy as:

- We **surrender** to God
- We **start trusting**
- We **stop sinning**
- We **stand firm**
- We **seek accountability**

How does faith change how we pursue victory in our personal lives? Faith *redefines* our ability to overcome and gives us a new set of tools to achieve personal victory.

It's possible to be victorious. It takes…

1. A continual surrender to God
2. A disciplined mind and body
3. An understanding of God's Word
4. A reliance on Christ's strength in us
5. A fair amount of leaning on friends

SUMMARY

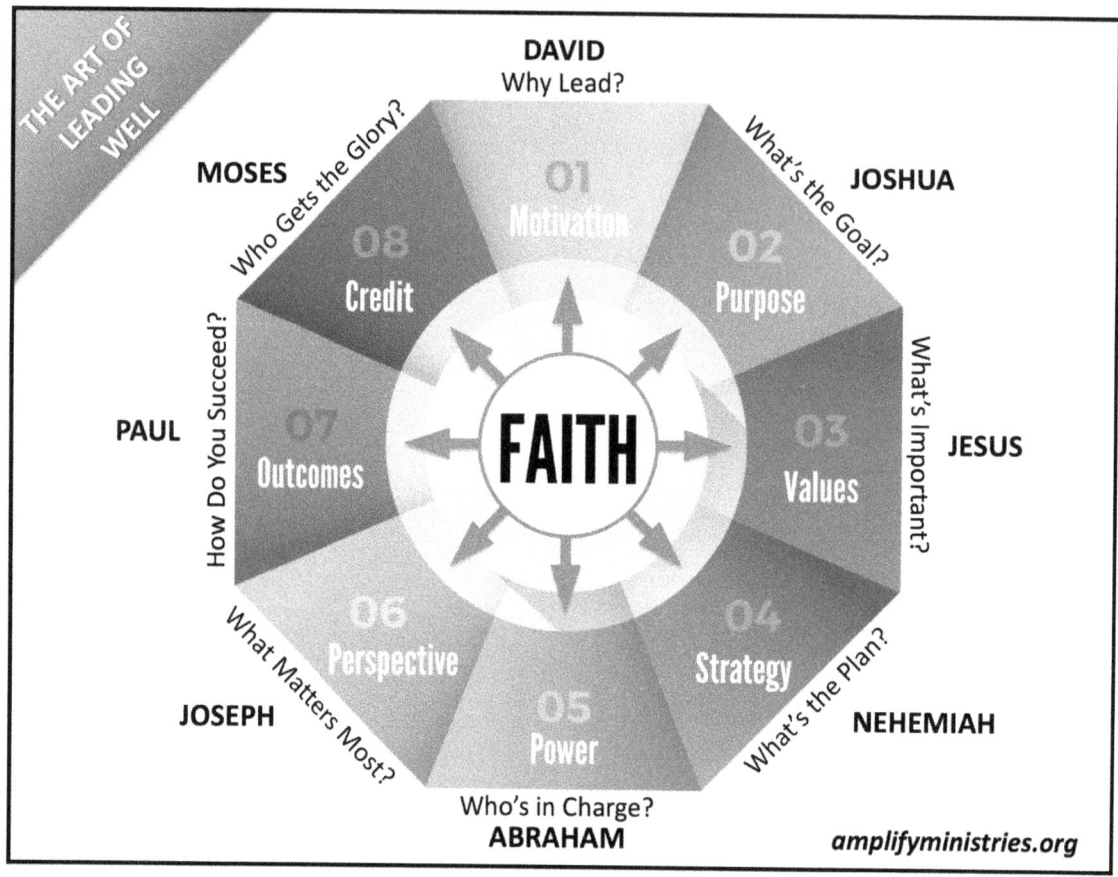

- Keep your faith at the center of your leadership. It will transform how you lead.
- Remember, leading well is a journey.
- Sometimes we'll get it right and sometimes we'll make mistakes.
- Keep trying to improve, develop, grow, and become a better leader than you were before.

THE WRAP UP

- We hope that you have grown in your understanding and ability to lead well.
- Find ways to apply these concepts in your leadership context and pass them on.
- Thanks for joining us and taking the time to develop your leadership and your faith.
- May God bless your leadership as you put His Word and these principles into practice.

THE APPLICATION: PUTTING IT INTO PRACTICE

- As we conclude this course, reflect on what you have learned. Think about, discuss, and apply the following questions one more time.

1. Which topic or featured leader impacted you the most? Why?

_____

_____

2. How has this course encouraged you in your leadership and faith journey?

_____

_____

3. What are 2-3 leadership principles that you hope to implement?

_____

_____

4. How can you share what you have learned with other leaders and teammates?

_____

_____

5. Who are some people you know who would benefit from this course?

_____

_____

6. How will your faith and the principles you have learned change the way you lead?

_____

_____

MY BIG TAKEAWAYS	1. _____
	2. _____
	3. _____

LEADERSHIP REBORN

Thanks for joining us!
Keep leading, keep serving, and keep loving those around you.

ADDITIONAL PRODUCTS
Leadership Reborn Resources

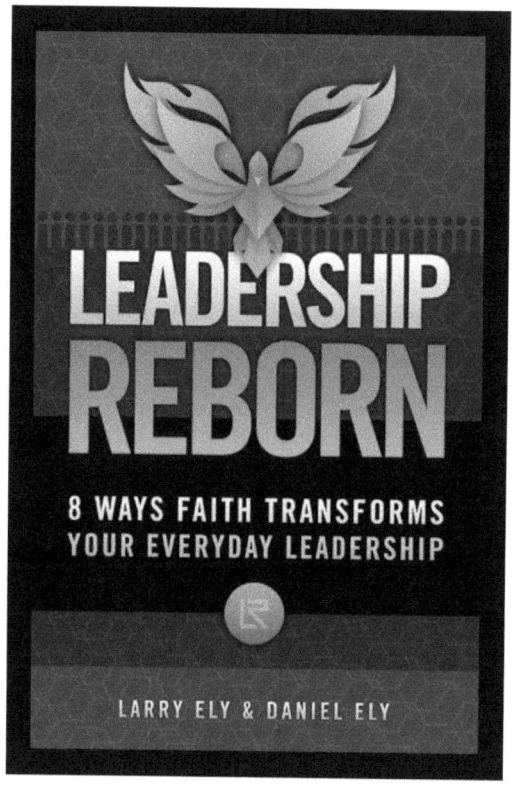

MAIN BOOK

Go deeper with the main book and dive into the details, backgrounds, and full stories of each chapter.

- **10 LEADERS** from the Bible with more details and deeper insight
- **10 FULL STORIES** illustrating leadership principles
- **10 FULL SPOTLIGHTS** highlighting leadership in action
- **NEW QUOTES** from interviews with leaders in the trenches
- **QUESTIONS** to discuss and help you grow

To order products, visit us online.

www.leadershipbooks.com

www.amplifyministries.org/leadership-reborn/

READING PLAN AND E-BOOK

- **READING PLAN:** 5-Day Bible Reading Plan based on the book to help leaders grow in their faith. This Leadership Devotional will be available in the Bible App.

- **E-BOOK:** A digital version of the main book will be available on most major reading platforms.

- To access available products, search Leadership Reborn in the related Apps.

Visit us online for more details.

www.amplifyministries.org/leadership-reborn/

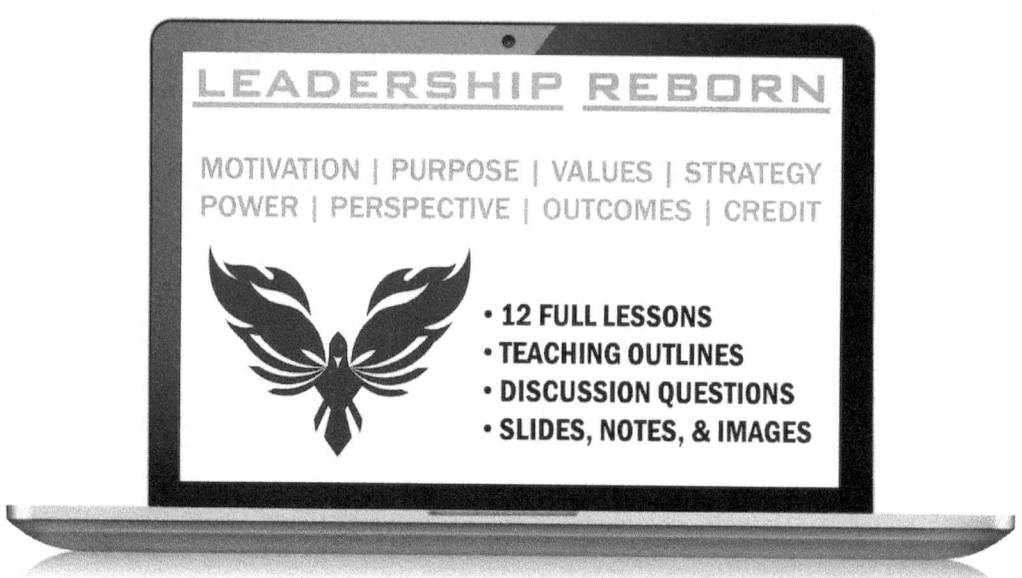

TEACHING SERIES

Would you like to teach this leadership content to your team, church, or company? Great! Here's a complete packaged resource to teach the book yourself.

- **TEACHING PACKAGE:** A 12-week message series will be available for leaders to teach the main book themselves. *(Series will include message notes, outlines, teaching slides, discussion questions, and graphics- all as a digital download).*

To order products, visit us online.
www.leadershipbooks.com
www.amplifyministries.org/leadership-reborn/

SPEAKING

Invite the author to speak at your next Leadership Training event. Larry Ely is available to book for speaking engagements and team training for churches, companies, schools, universities, retreats, youth groups, workshops, seminars, and conferences.

For booking, visit us online.

www.leadershipbooks.com/pages/larry-and-dan-ely-speakers-bureau
www.amplifyministries.org/leadership-reborn/

STAY CONNECTED

Keep up to date with the authors.

- **WEB**: www.amplifyministries.org
- **YOUTUBE**: www.youtube.com/@amplifystudentministries
- **INSTAGRAM**: @amplify_ministries
- **FACEBOOK**: www.facebook.com
  (Search "Leadership Reborn" for our Group Page)

LEADERSHIP CHALLENGE

You are invited to join the **"5 Day Leadership Challenge."**
Take 5 MINUTES for 5 DAYS to improve and sharpen your leadership. It's EASY to participate. Simply: Read, Comment, and Share.

- **READ** the daily article
- **COMMENT** on a key aspect
- **SHARE** it with a friend or teammate

CHECK IT OUT: www.amplifyministries.org/leadership-challenge/

NOTES

Session 1:

[1] Nicole P. Vogt, "ASTR 110G Introduction to Astronomy: Geocentric and Heliocentric Models," *New Mexico State University*, 2006, accessed August 22, 2023, http://astronomy.nmsu.edu/nicole/teaching/ASTR110/lectures/quickview.html.

Session 2:

[1] "National Football League," "Super Bowl," "NFL," and *Green Bay Packers* are all trademarks of the National Football League and/or National Football League Properties, 2024.

[2] Vince Lombardi Jr, *What It Takes to Be #1: Vince Lombardi on Leadership* (New York, NY: McGraw-Hill, 2001), 132.

[3] "John F. Kennedy and PT-109," *John F. Kennedy Presidential Library and Museum*, accessed March 1, 2023, https://www.jfklibrary.org/learn/about-jfk/jfk-in-history/john-f-kennedy-and-pt-109.

[4] William Doyle, *PT 109: An American Epic of War, Survival, and the Destiny of John F. Kennedy* (New York, NY: Harper Collins Publishers, 2015).

Session 3:

[1] Jim Lovell and Jeffrey Kluger, *Lost Moon: The Perilous Voyage of Apollo 13,* (New York, NY: Houghton Mifflin Harcourt Publishing, 1994).

[2] Ron Howard (Director), 1995. *Apollo 13* [Film]. Universal Pictures.

[3] Taylor University, "Taylor: A Magazine for Taylor University Alumni, Parents and Friends (Summer 2021)" (2021). Article "Breakthrough." *The Taylor Magazine (1963-Present)*. 195. (p.31-21), accessed October 11, 2022, https://pillars.taylor.edu/tu_magazines/195.

Session 4:

[1] Stephen Lambert (Creator), 2010-2022. *Undercover Boss* [TV Series], Network: CBS.

[2] Curt Fowler, "Core 4 Leadership at Chick-fil-A," *Values Driven Results with Curt Fowler,* 2016, accessed September 5, 2022, https://valuesdrivenresults.com/newsletter/core-4-leadership-chick-fil-exercise-joints-amazing-story-forgiveness/.

[3] Chick-fil-A 405 at Jefferson (Los Angeles, CA), "Team Member Opportunity Guide: Core Four," *CFA405jefferson,* accessed April 26, 2023, https://www.cfa405jefferson.com/team-member-opportunity-guide.

Session 5:

[1] Åke Sandberg, "Enriching Production: Perspectives on Volvo›s Uddevalla Plant as an Alternative to Lean Production," *Industrial and Labor Relations Review,* Vol. 50, February, 1995, downloaded December 2, 2022, https://www.researchgate.net/publication/23543035_Enriching_Production_ Perspectives_on_Volvo%27s_Uddevalla_Plant_as_an_Alternative_to_Lean_Production.

[2] Ibid., 108.

Session 6:

[1] James S. Hewett, *Illustrations Unlimited* (Wheaton, IL: Tyndale House Publishers, Inc, 1988), 102-103.

[2] "Infamous Company Power Struggles," *Pack and Send,* 2015, accessed March 22, 2023, https://www.packsend.co.uk/infamous-company-power-struggles/.

[3] Alex Sherman, "Extremely Awkward: Bob Chapek and Bob Iger Had a Falling Out… Rift Looms Over Disney's Future," *CNBC*, March 2022, accessed March 22, 2023, https://www.cnbc.com/2022/ 03/20/disney-ceo-chapek-iger-falling-out.html.

[4] Mike Calia and Alex Sherman, "Bob Iger Returns as Disney CEO, Replacing Bob Chapek After a Brief, Tumultuous Tenure," *CNBC*, November 2022, accessed March 22, 2023, https://www.cnbc.com/2022/11/21/bob-iger-named-disney-ceo-effective-immediately.html.

Session 7:

[1] Barry R. Masters, "History of the Optical Microscope in Cell Biology and Medicine," *Encyclopedia of Life Sciences: ELS* (Chichester, UK: John Wiley and Sons, Ltd., September, 2008, downloaded December 1, 2022), 1-2.

[2] Henry C. King, *The History of the Telescope* (Mineola, NY: Dover Publications, Inc. 2003,1979,1955), 30-38.

[3] Diane Tedeschi, "The Planet Detective," *Air and Space Quarterly*, (Washington, DC: Smithsonian National Air and Space Museum, Fall 2022), 25-39.

[4] Susan Bell, "A Cosmic Conversation," *USC Dornsife Magazine: The Cosmos Issue* (Los Angeles, CA: University of Southern California, Fall 2021-Winter 2022), 17-20.

[5] Harry V. Jaffa, *A New Birth of Freedom: Abraham Lincoln and the Coming of the Civil War* (Lanham, MD: Rowman and Littlefield Publishers, Inc., 2004), 259.

[6] Abraham Lincoln, Don E. Fehrenbacher (Annotator), *Selected Speeches and Writings: Abraham Lincoln* (New York, NY: First Vintage Books, Library of America, 1992).

[7] Don E. and Virginia E. Fehrenbacher (Editors), *Recollected Words of Abraham Lincoln* (Redwood City, CA: Stanford University Press, 1996), 330-331.

[8] Justin Ewers, "Abraham Lincoln's Great Awakening: From Moderate to Abolitionist." *U.S. News and World Report*, February 9, 2009.

[9] Doris K. Goodwin, *Leadership in Turbulent Times*, (New York, NY: Simon and Schuster, 2018).

[10] Michael Burlingame, *Abraham Lincoln: A Life*, (Baltimore, MD: Johns Hopkins University Press, 2008).

Session 8:

[1] Team Tony, "The Determination of Shaun White: Unlocking Greatness in the Face of Failures and Obstacles," *Tony Robbins Podcast: Shaun White's Ultimate Redemption*, January 10, 2019, accessed March 6, 2023, https://www-tonyrobins.com/podcasts/shaun-whites-ultimate/redemption/.

[2] "Shaun White: Olympic Gold Medalist and Entrepreneur," *Leading Authorities, Inc.*, accessed March 6, 2023, https://www.leadingauthorities.com/speakers/shaun-white.

[3] John Branch, "Sometimes Shaun White's Troubles Start When He's 20 Feet in the Air," *The New York Times*, February 8, 2022, accessed March 6, 2023, https://www.nytimes.com/2022/02/08/ sports/olympics/shaun-white-olympics-snowboard.html.

[4] Quentin Reynolds, *The Wright Brothers: Pioneers of American Aviation* (New York, NY: Landmark Books, Random House Pub.), 1950.

[5] G.D. Padfield and B. Lawrence, "The Birth of Flight: An Engineering Analysis of the Wright Brothers 1902 Glider," *The Aeronautical Journal* (Liverpool, UK: The University of Liverpool, December, 2003), 697-718.

Session 9:

[1] John W. Dean, *Blind Ambition: The White House Years* (New York, NY: Simon and Schuster, 1976), 150-151.

[2] John W. Dean, *Blind Ambition: The End of the Story* (Palm Springs, CA: Polimedia Publishing, 2009).

[3] Phil Vischer, "General Session #1: Phil Vischer," *National Youth Workers Convention* (Cincinnati, OH: Youth Specialties, 2006.

Session 10:

[1] "The Best Betrayals in Movies: #4 Joseph D. Pistone in Donnie Brasco," *Fandango,* accessed January 11, 2022, https://www.fandango.com/movie-photos/the-best-betrayals-in-movies-355.

Session 11:

[1] Sarah Pruitt, "Why Does the Leaning Tower of Pisa Lean?" *HISTORY A&E Television Networks, LLC.,* 2015, accessed January 31, 2023, https://www.history.com/news/why-does-the-leaning-tower-of-pisa-lean.

www.ingramcontent.com/pod-product-compliance
Lightning Source LLC
Chambersburg PA
CBHW041118120626

46547CB00019B/2762